The Pilgrim's Guide

The Pilgrim's Guide

A 12th Century Guide for the Pilgrim to
St James of Compostella

Translated from the Latin by
James Hogarth

Confraternity of St James

Published by:
The Confraternity of St James
45, Dolben St, London, SE1 OUQ.

© Confraternity of St James 1992
ISBN 1 870585 11 9

Typeset in Pembroke 12pt by Barry Humpidge on an Acorn Archimedes computer using Impression II software by Computer Concepts Ltd. Printed on the presses of the Monteney Community Workshop, Sheffield. Bound by Hammond Bindery, Limited, Wakefield.

CONTENTS

Introduction vii
Stages on the Road to St James xiii
The Pilgrim's Guide 1
Appendix: Modern guides for the Pilgrim 89
Index 91

Illustrations

Plan of the old city 61
Plan of the Romanesque Cathedral 64
Plan of the modern Cathedral 65
Map .... inside back cover

Acknowledgements

Many thanks to Mollie Coviello, for the stalwart Pilgrim on the title page, and Margaret Gray and Angela Lauener for the map.

Thanks also to the following for permission to reproduce copyright material:

Harrap Publishing Group Ltd and Luis Miguel Pulgar for the plan of the Cathedral of Santiago as it now is, from *'Santiago de Compostela (Everything Under the Sun)'*, London, 1988.

Harvard University Press and K. J. Conant for the plan of the cathedral as it was in the 12th Century, from *'The Early Architectural History of the Cathedral of Santiago de Compostela'*, Cambridge, Mass. 1926.

Plan of the City of Santiago de Compostela according to Juan Uría, based on that of Meyer, from p.407, vol.II of Luis Vázquez de Parga, José María Lacarra, and Juan Uría Ríu, *Las Peregrinaciones a Santiago de Compostela*, Madrid, 1945.

Introduction

The shrine of St James at Compostella (Santiago de Compostela) in Galicia, at the remote north-western corner of Spain, which is believed to contain the remains of the apostle, has been the goal of pilgrims for more than a thousand years.

Although there is no reference in apostolic times to the evangelisation of Spain by James, there is evidence in the 6th, 7th and 8th centuries of a tradition that James did preach the Gospel there; and confirmation of the tradition was seen in the miraculous discovery of his tomb early in the 9th century: the exact date is not known, but it was probably about 813. A hermit named Pelayo claimed to have received an angelic revelation that St James was buried on the hill where the city of Compostella now stands and to have seen a bright star shining over it. He informed the local bishop, Theodomir of Iria Flavia (now Padrón), who went to the spot indicated by the star, discovered an ancient tomb and declared that it was that of the Apostle.

The discovery was reported to the Pope (Leo III), who proclaimed it to the whole Christian world. A church was built over the tomb by King Alfonso II of Asturias (which then included León and Galicia), and pilgrims began to flock to the shrine. Later the original modest church was replaced by a grander one, which became a cathedral when the episcopal see was moved from Iria Flavia to Compostella. To explain the presence of the saint's tomb in Galicia a legend grew up that after his return to Palestine from his evangelising mission in Spain and his execution by Herod (Acts 12,2) his disciples recovered his body, took it down to the coast, from which, with the saint's body, they were miraculously transported in an unmanned boat to the Galician coast at what is now Padrón.

Thereafter the numbers of pilgrims making their way from all over Christendom to St James's shrine at Compostella continued to increase. In course of time numbers of religious houses providing accommodation for pilgrims were built along the route, roads were improved and bridges were built to ease the pilgrims' journey. As a result there came into being a recognised pilgrim road along northern Spain from the Pyrenees to Compostella, known as the Camino de Santiago (Way of St James), or Camino Francés (French Road) since it was travelled by pilgrims coming from or through France. Within France too there were particularly favoured routes along which pilgrims travelled from different parts of France and other countries in Europe to join the French Road in Spain.

The 'Pilgrim's Guide' was written in the 12th century, probably around 1140-50. It is the earliest of the many descriptions that have come down to us of the pilgrimage to the shrine of St James. Unlike other accounts, however, it is not primarily a description of one particular pilgrim's journey—though it is clearly based on personal experience and is strongly imbued with the author's feelings and prejudices—but is designed to help prospective pilgrims with advice and guidance for their journey.

The 'Guide' is contained in a 12th century Latin manuscript known as the Codex Calixtinus, after an apocryphal letter attributed to Pope Calixtus or Callistus II (d. 1124) which serves as a kind of preface, or more familiarly as the 'Book of St James' *(Liber Sancti Jacobi)*. This was a compilation evidently designed to promote the pilgrimage to Compostella, no doubt under the influence of Diego Gelmírez (bishop of Compostella from 1100, archbishop from 1120), an energetic and ambitious prelate who actively promoted the development of the pilgrimage, the building of the new cathedral which had been begun by his predecessor Diego Peláez, and the enhancement of Compostella's (and his own) status.

There are four versions of the Codex Calixtinus, the finest of which is preserved in the archives of Santiago Cathedral. It consists of five books, of different origins and dates. The first and longest of the books is an anthology of hymns, sermons and liturgical writings in honour of St James; the second is a collection of miracles attributed to the saint, most of them fairly recent (i.e. dating from the early years of the 12th century); the third is an account of the evangelisation of Spain by St James, his martyrdom and the transfer of his remains from Jerusalem to Compostella; the fourth is devoted to the 'History of Charlemagne and Roland', the story (attributed to Charlemagne's warlike Archbishop Turpin) of Charlemagne's legendary expeditions into Spain, linking the epic of the Emperor and his paladins with the story of St James and the pilgrimage to Compostella; and the fifth consists of the 'Pilgrim's Guide'. (In the manuscript preserved in Santiago the

'History of Charlemagne and Roland' was detached and bound separately in the 18th century, so that in this text the 'Guide' is described as the fourth book.)

Although generally dated to around 1140-50, the 'Pilgrim's Guide' appears to be a compilation including work by more than one hand, written at different dates. Its author or compiler is not positively known, but the work is commonly attributed to one Aimery (Aymericus) Picaud, a cleric from Parthenay-le-Vieux in Poitou, who may have travelled to Compostella in the retinue of a noble lady named Gerberga or Gebirga. Certainly the author seems to have been a Frenchman, writing his guide—in Latin—primarily for the benefit of French pilgrims; and the text of the Guide reflects the strong local patriotism of a native of Poitou and his distaste for the manners and customs of practically all the other peoples encountered on the road to Compostella. He may or may not have been the same person as one Aymericus who was a papal chancellor in the mid 12th century. To give greater authority to the 'Guide' certain chapters are specifically attributed to Pope Callistus, Aimery or Aimery the Chancellor.

The Guide is divided into eleven chapters, the longest of which are the seventh, eighth and ninth, devoted respectively to the characteristics of the countries and the peoples on the road to Compostella, the shrines to be visited on the way (particularly in France, with a long excursus on the life and passion of St Eutrope of Saintes) and a description of the town and cathedral of Compostella. The exact route is outlined in two shorter chapters, the second and the third.

The second chapter of the Guide divides the journey to Santiago from the French frontier into thirteen stages, as shown in the table on page xiii. The rationale of this subdivision is not clear. It appears to imply that each stage represents a day's journey; but it seems unlikely that even a well mounted group of pilgrims—with which the author of the Guide must be presumed to have travelled, though only two of the stages are specifically described as being done on horseback—could complete a journey of between 440 and 490 miles, with stages of up to 60 miles, in only thirteen days. A modern pilgrim[1] took twenty-three riding days for the journey, with a maximum day's journey of 30 miles and an average speed over the whole distance of just under 3½ miles an hour. Is it possible that the author of the Guide mentions only staging-points which he is anxious to recommend because at these places there were religious houses or hospices run by a religious order with which he had affiliations (perhaps the Cluniac order which played a major part in organising the pilgrim route and is particularly mentioned in the envoi to the Guide)?

* * * * *

Any reader or translator of the 'Pilgrim's Guide' must owe a great debt to Mademoiselle Jeanne Vielliard

---

[1] Robin Hanbury-Tenison, *Spanish Pilgrimage: a Canter to St James*, London, Hutchinson, 1990; paperback edition, Arrow Books, 1991.

for her excellent edition of the Latin text[2], accompanied by a French translation. Her edition is based on the Santiago manuscript, with variants from a manuscript from the monastery of Ripoll in Catalonia, now held in the Archives of the Crown of Aragon in Barcelona. The present translator has also profited from the recent German and Spanish editions by Klaus Herbers[3] and Millán Bravo Lozano[4].

There are a number of obscurities in the text and some minor variations between the Santiago and Ripoll texts, leaving room for differences of interpretation. Where, in such cases, there is a general consensus about the meaning, it is followed in this translation without comment; one or two cases of particular difficulty are discussed in footnotes.

James Hogarth
Edinburgh
1992

---

[2] Jeanne Vielliard, *Le Guide du Pèlerin de Saint-Jacques de Compostelle*, 5th ed., Paris, Librairie Philosophique J. Vrin, 1984.

[3] Klaus Herbers, *Der Jakobsweg*, 2nd ed., Tübingen, Gunter Narr Verlag, 1986.

[4] Millán Bravo Lozano, *Guía del Peregrino Medieval*, Sahagún, Centro de Estudios del Camino de Santiago, 1989.

STAGES ON THE ROAD TO ST JAMES

From	To	Km	Miles

Borce (via Somport) to Puente la Reina
1 Borce	Jaca	36	22.4
2 Jaca	Monreal	97.5	60.6
3 Monreal	Puente la Reina	24.7	15.3
Borce to Santiago		782	486

San Michel (via Ibañeta) to Santiago
1 Saint-Michel	Viscarret	21.5	13.3
2 Viscarret	Pamplona	28.5	17.7
3 Pamplona (via Puente la Reina)	Estella	43	26.7
4 Estella	Nájera	69	42.9
5 Nájera	Burgos	85	52.8
6 Burgos	Frómista	59	36.7
7 Frómista	Sahagún	55.5	34.5
8 Sahagún	León	52.5	32.6
9 León	Rabanal	64.3	40
10 Rabanal	Villafranca	49.5	30.8
11 Villafranca	Triacastela	47.2	29.3
12 Triacastela	Palas de Rey	58.5	36.4
13 Palas de Rey	Santiago	63	39
Saint-Michel to Santiago		712	442

The distances in kilometres are taken from Eusebio Goicoechea Arrondo, *Rutas Jacobeas*, Estella, 1971.

HERE BEGINS THE FOURTH BOOK OF SAINT JAMES THE APOSTLE

By the blessed Pope Callistus

> If the instructed reader seeks truth in our works let him take up this book without hesitation, for many people still living can bear witness that what is written in it is true.

The Pilgrim Guide[5]

Chapter I.	Of the Roads to St James	[page 3]
Chapter II.	Of the Stages on the Road to St James	[page 5]
Chapter III.	Of the Names of Places on the Road	[page 7]
Chapter IV.	Of the three good houses in the world	[page 9]
Chapter V.	Of the names of the road-makers of St James	[page 11]
Chapter VI.	Of the Bitter and the Sweet waters on the Road	[page 13]
Chapter VII.	Of the Characteristics of the Lands and the Peoples on the Road	[page 17]
Chapter VIII.	Of the Bodies of the Saints to be seen on the Roads to St James and of the Passion of St Eutropius	[page 27]
Chapter IX.	Of the Characteristics of the City and the Church of St James	[page 59]
Chapter X.	Of the Distribution of the offerings to the altar of St James	[page 85]
Chapter XI.	Of the fitting Reception to be given to Pilgrims of St James	[page 87]

---

5 This 'Table of Contents' was added when the 'History of Charlemagne and Roland' was separated from the rest of the 'Book of St James'. The chapter headings do not correspond exactly to those used in the body of the text.

Chapter I
Of the Roads to St James

There are four roads leading to St James which join to form one road at Puente la Reina, in the territory of Spain. One runs by way of St Giles [Saint-Gilles du Gard] and Montpellier and Toulouse and the Somport pass; another by St Mary of Le Puy and St Faith of Conques and St Peter of Moissac; the third by St Mary Magdalene of Vézelay and St Leonard of Limousin [Saint-Léonard de Noblat] and the town of Périgueux; and the fourth by St Martin of Tours and St Hilary of Poitiers and St John of Angély [Saint-Jean d'Angély] and St Eutropius of Saintes and the town of Bordeaux.

The roads which go by St Faith, by St Leonard and by St Martin join at Ostabat and after crossing the pass of Cize[6] meet the road over the Somport pass at Puente la Reina; and from there a single road leads to St James.

---

6 The Cize is the upper valley of the river Nive, with Saint-Jean-Pied-de-Port as its chief place. The pass of Cize is the passage through the Pyrenees between the Nive valley and Roncesvalles—probably, at the time the Guide was written, following the old crest road via Leizar-Athéka and the Collado Lepoeder rather than the valley road by way of Valcarlos. The crest road was preferred in the early days of the pilgrimage, since the wooded valley road, exposing travellers to ambush and attack by robbers, was then regarded as less safe.

3

Chapter II

Of the Stages on the Road to St James

Pope Callistus

From the Somport pass to Puente la Reina there are three short stages. The first is from Borce, which is a village at the foot of the Somport pass on the Gascon side, to Jaca; the second from Jaca to Monreal; the third from Monreal to Puente la Reina.

From the pass of Cize to St James there are thirteen stages. The first is from the village of Saint-Michel, which is at the foot of the pass of Cize on the Gascon side, to Viscarret, and this is a short stage. The second is from Viscarret to Pamplona, and this too is a short stage. The third is from the town of Pamplona to Estella. The fourth, done on horseback, is from Estella to the town of Nájera. The fifth, also on horseback, is from Nájera to the town of Burgos. The sixth is from Burgos to Frómista. The seventh is from Frómista to St Facundus [Sahagún]. The eighth is from St Facundus to the town of León. The ninth is from León to Rabanal. The tenth is from Rabanal over the pass of Monte Irago [Foncebadón] to Villafranca del Bierzo, at the mouth of the Valcarce. The eleventh is from Villafranca over the pass of Monte Cebrero to Triacastela. The twelfth is from Triacastela to Palas de Rey. The thirteenth is from Palas de Rey to St James, and this is a short stage.

Chapter III

Of the Names of the Places on the Road to St James

From the Somport pass to Puente la Reina these are the places on the road to St James: first there is Borce, at the foot of the mountains on the Gascon side; then, after going over the highest point in the mountains, the hospice of Santa Cristina; then Canfranc; then Jaca; then Astorito; then Tiermas, with royal baths in which the water is always hot; then Monreal; then Puente la Reina.

From the pass of Cize, on the Way of St James, to his church in Galicia these are the most important places: first the village of Saint-Michel, at the foot of the pass of Cize on the Gascon side; then, after going over the highest point in the mountains, the Hospice of Roland [the monastery of Roncesvalles]; then the village of Roncesvalles [Burguete]; then Viscarret; then Larrasoaña; then the town of Pamplona; then Puente la Reina; then Estella, which is fertile in good bread and excellent wine and meat and fish and full of all delights; then Los Arcos, Logroño, Villarroya, the town of Nájera, Santo Domingo [de la Calzada], Redecilla, Belorado, Villafranca, the forest of Oca, Atapuerca, the town of Burgos, Tardajos, Hornillos del Camino, Castrojeriz, the Puente de Itero and Frómista; then Carrión, which is an industrious and prosperous town, rich in bread and wine and meat and all fruitfulness; then St Facundus [Sahagún], overflowing with all delights, with a meadow in which, so it is said, the gleaming lances of the victorious warriors, set in the ground to glorify God, once put forth leaves.

Then there are Mansilla and the town of León, residence of the king and the court, full of all delights; then Orbigo, the town of Astorga and Rabanal, known as the Captive[7]; then the pass of Monte Irago [Foncebadón], Molinaseca, Ponferrada, Cacabelos and Villafranca del Bierzo, at the mouth of the Valcarce; then the Castle of the Saracens[8] and Villa Us[9]; then the pass of Monte Cebrero, with a hospice on the highest point of the mountain; then Linares de Rey and Triacastela, at the foot of this mountain in Galicia, where pilgrims pick up a stone and carry it to Castañeda to make lime for the building of the Apostle's church. Then there are the village of San Miguel[10], Barbadelo, the bridge over the Miño [Puertomarín], Sala de la Reina[11], Palas de Rey, Leboreiro, Santiago de Boente, Castañeda, Villanova, Ferreiros and finally Compostella, the most excellent city of the Apostle, overflowing with all delights, having in its care the precious body of St James—for which it is recognised to be the most fortunate and most noble of all the cities of Spain.

I have briefly described these places and the stages on the road so that pilgrims setting out for St James may be able to estimate the expenses involved in their journey.

---

7 The origin of this epithet is unknown; possibly a corruption of a Galician word meaning 'small'.
8 Unidentified.
9 Perhaps Herrerías (E. Valiña Sampedro, *El Camino de Santiago: Estudio histórico-jurídico*. Lugo, 1990, pp 122-123).
10 Apparently near Sarria.   11 Unidentified.

Chapter IV
Of the World's Three Hospices

The Lord established in this world three columns most necessary for the support of the poor: the hospice in Jerusalem, the hospice of Mont-Joux [on the Great St Bernard pass] and the hospice of Santa Cristina on the Somport pass. These hospices were sited in places where they were necessary: they are holy places, houses of God, places of refreshment for holy pilgrims, of rest for the needy, of comfort for the sick, of salvation for the dead, of help for the living. Those who built these most holy places will without doubt possess the kingdom of God.

Chapter V

Of the Names of those who repaired the Road to St James

Aimery

These are the names of those who, in the time of Diego [Gelmírez], archbishop of St James, and Alfonso, emperor of Spain and Galicia, and Pope Callistus, repaired the road to St James, from Rabanal to Puertomarín, for the love of God and His Apostle, before the year 1120, in the reign of Alfonso [I] of Aragón and Louis [VI] le Gros, king of France: Andrew, Roger, Avitus, Fortus, Arnold, Stephen and Peter, who rebuilt the bridge over the Miño which had been demolished by Queen Urraca. May the souls of these men and those who worked with them rest in eternal peace!

Chapter VI

Of the Good and the Bad Rivers on the Road to St James

Pope Callistus

These are the rivers on the road to St James from the pass of Cize and the Somport pass. From the Somport pass there flows down a river of pure water, the Aragón, which irrigates Spain. From the pass of Cize there flows a river of pure water which many call the Runa[12] and which flows down towards Pamplona. At Puente la Reina there are both the Arga and the Runa. At a place called Lorca, to the east, there flows a stream known as the Salt River. Beware of drinking from it or of watering your horse in it, for this river brings death. On its banks, while we were going to St James, we found two Navarrese sitting there sharpening their knives; for they are accustomed to flay pilgrims' horses which die after drinking the water. In answer to our question they lied, saying that the water was good and drinkable. Accordingly we watered our horses in the river, and at once two of them died and were forthwith skinned by the two men.

Through Estella flows the river Ega, the water of which is sweet, pure and excellent. At the village of Los

---

12 Another name for the Arga?

Arcos is a stream[13] which brings death, and between Los Arcos and the first hospice beyond the village is another stream which is fatal to both horses and men who drink it. At the village of Torres del Río, in Navarrese territory, is a river which also is fatal to horses and men; and there is another river that brings death at the village of Cuevas[14].

At Logroño is a large river called the Ebro, with pure water and an abundance of fish. All the rivers between Estella and Logroño have water which brings death to men and beasts who drink it, and the fish in these streams are likewise poisonous. Do not eat, in Spain or Galicia, the fish commonly known as *barbus* [barbel], or the one which the Poitevins call *alose* [shad] and the Italians *clipia*, or an eel or a tench: if you do you will assuredly die or fall sick. And anyone who eats any great quantity of these and does not fall sick must have a stronger constitution than other people or must have lived in the country for a long time; for all kinds of fish, beef and pork in Spain and Galicia make foreigners ill.

Those rivers which are sweet and good for drinking are the following: the Pisuerga, which flows at the Puente de Itero; the Carrión, at Carrión de los Condes; the Cea at Sahagún; the Esla at Mansilla de las Mulas; the Porma, at the large bridge [the Puente de Villarente] between Mansilla and León; the Torio, which flows through León, below the Jewish quarter; the Bernesga, on the far side of León in the direction of Astorga; the Sil at Ponferrada, in a green valley; the Cúa at Cacabelos; the Burbia at the bridge of Villafranca del

---

13 The Río Odrón.
14 An outlying district of Viana. The river is the Presa.

Bierzo; the Valcarce, which flows down the valley of that name; the Miño at Puertomarín; and a river in wooded country two miles from the city of St James, at a place called Lavacolla[15], in which French pilgrims travelling to St James are accustomed, for love of the Apostle, to take off their clothes and cleanse not only their private parts but the whole of their body. The river Sar, which flows between the Mount of Joy [Monte del Gozo] and the city of St James, is held to be clean; so too is the Sarela, which flows on the other side of the town, to the west.

I have described these rivers so that pilgrims going to St James may take care to avoid drinking bad water and may choose water that is good for them and for their horses.

---

15 The present-day name of Lavacolla probably originally had the same significance as the Latin name used in the guide; Lavamentula (*mentula* = private parts).

Chapter VII

Of the Names of the Countries and the Characteristics of the Peoples on the Road to St James

Going to St James on the Toulouse road, we come first, after crossing the Garonne, into Gascony, and then, going over the Somport pass, enter Aragon and then Navarre, which extends as far as the bridge over the Arga [Puente la Reina] and beyond. If, however, we take the road over the pass of Cize we come, after Tours, into Poitou, a fertile and excellent region, full of all delights. The men of Poitou are strong and warlike, skilled in the use of bows and arrows and of lances in war, valiant in battle, swift runners, elegant in their attire, handsome of face, ready of tongue, generous and hospitable. Then comes Saintonge; and from there, after crossing an arm of the sea and the river Garonne, we come into the territory of Bordeaux, which has excellent wine and an abundance of fish but an uncouth manner of speech. The speech of Saintonge is also uncouth, but that of Bordeaux is more so.

Then, for travellers who are already tired, there is a three days' journey through the Landes of Bordeaux.

This is a desolate country, lacking in everything: there is neither bread nor wine nor meat nor fish nor water nor any springs. There are few villages on this sandy plain, though it has honey, millet, panic[16] and pigs in plenty. If you are going through the Landes in summer be sure to protect your face from the huge flies, called *guespe* [wasps] and *tavones* [horse-flies], which are particularly abundant in this region. And if you do not watch your feet carefully you will sink up to your knees in the sea sand which is found everywhere here.

After passing through this region you come into Gascony, a land well supplied with white bread and excellent red wine, woods and meadows, rivers and springs of pure water. The Gascons are loud-mouthed, talkative, given to mockery, libidinous, drunken, greedy eaters, clad in rags and poverty-stricken; but they are skilled fighters and notable for their hospitality to the poor. They take their meals without a table, sitting round the fire, and all drink out of the same cup. They eat and drink a great deal and are ill clad; nor do they scruple to sleep all together on a scanty litter of rotting straw, the servants along with the master and mistress.

Leaving this country, the road to St James crosses two rivers near the village of Saint-Jean de Sorde, one on the right and the other on the left; one is called a *gave*, the other a river, and they must both be crossed by boat. Accursed be their boatmen! For although the rivers are quite narrow these men are in the habit of taking a piece of money[17] for each person, rich or poor,

---

16 A kind of millet.
17 Latin *nummus*, value unspecified; probably a French denier, a penny.

whom they ferry across, and for a horse they exact four, unworthily and by force. Their boat is small, made from a single tree-trunk, ill suited to carry horses; and so when you get into the boat you must take care not to fall into the water. You will do well to hold on to your horse's bridle and let it swim behind the boat. Nor should you go into a boat that has too many passengers, for if it is overloaded it will at once capsize.

Often, too, having taken their passengers' money, the boatmen take such a number of other pilgrims on board that the boat overturns and the pilgrims are drowned; and then the wicked boatmen are delighted and appropriate the possessions of the dead.

Then, round the pass of Cize, is the Basque country, with the town of Bayonne on the coast to the north. Here a barbarous tongue is spoken; the country is wooded and hilly, short of bread, wine and all other foodstuffs, except only apples, cider and milk. In this country there are wicked toll-collectors—near the pass of Cize and at Ostabat and Saint-Jean and Saint-Michel-Pied-de-Port—may they be accursed! They come out to meet pilgrims with two or three cudgels to exact tribute by improper use of force; and if any traveller refuses to give the money they demand they strike him with their cudgels and take the money, abusing him and rummaging in his very breeches. They are ruthless people, and their country is no less hostile, with its forests and its wildness; the ferocity of their aspect and the barbarousness of their language strike terror into the hearts of those who encounter them. Although they should levy tribute only on merchants they exact it unjustly from pilgrims and all travellers. When custom requires that the duty to be paid on a particular object is four or six pieces of money they charge eight or twelve—double the proper amount.

We urge and demand, therefore, that these toll-collectors, together with the king of Aragon and the other rich men who receive the proceeds of the tolls and all those who are in league with them, to wit Raymond de Soule, Vivien d'Aigremont and the Vicomte de Saint-Michel, with all their posterity, and also the ferrymen already mentioned and Arnauld de la Guigne, with his posterity, and the other lords of the two rivers, who unjustly receive the money collected by the ferrymen, and also the priests who, knowing what they do, admit them to confession and the Eucharist, celebrate divine service for them and receive them in church—we demand that all these men should be excommunicated until they have expiated their offences by a long and public penance and have moderated their demands for tribute, and that the sentence of excommunication should be made public not only in their own episcopal see but also in the basilica of St James, in presence of the pilgrims. And if any prelate should pardon them, either from benevolence or for his own profit, may he be struck with the sword of anathema!

It should be said that the toll-collectors are not entitled to levy any kind of tribute on pilgrims and that the ferrymen are properly entitled to charge only an obol[18] for taking over two men—that is, if they are rich—and for a horse a piece of money; for a poor man they may charge nothing at all. Moreover the ferrymen

---

18 Worth half a denier or penny, the coin described as a 'piece of money'.

are required to have boats amply large enough to accommodate both men and horses.

Still in the Basque country, the road to St James goes over a most lofty mountain known as the Portus Cisere [Pass of Cize], so called either because it is the gateway of Spain or because necessary goods are transported over the pass from one country to the other[19]. It is a journey of eight miles up to the pass and another eight down from it. The mountain is so high that it seems to touch the sky, and a man who has climbed it feels that he could indeed reach the sky with his hand. From the summit can be seen the Sea of Brittany and the Western Sea, and the bounds of the three countries of Castile, Aragon and France. On the highest point of the mountain is the place known as the Cross of Charles, because it was here that Charlemagne, advancing into Spain with his armies, cleared a passage with the aid of axes and picks and mattocks and other implements, set up the Lord's cross and, kneeling with his face turned towards Galicia, prayed to God and St James. And so pilgrims are accustomed to kneel here in prayer, looking towards the country of St James, and each then sets up a cross. Sometimes as many as a thousand crosses are to be seen here, and so the place is known as the first station for prayer on the road to St James[20].

---

19 Explanations suggested by the similarity between *portus, porta* and *portare*.

20 In modern tradition the pass of Ibañeta has been regarded as the place where Charlemagne set up his cross, symbolised by the cross beside the modern chapel. But this is by no means 'the highest point of the mountain': there are much wider

On this mountain, before Christianity was fully established in Spain, the impious Navarrese and the Basques were accustomed not only to rob pilgrims going to St James but to ride them like asses and kill them. Near the mountain, to the north, is a valley known as the Valley of Charles [Valcarlos], in which Charlemagne was encamped with his armies when his warriors were killed at Roncesvalles. This is the road used by many pilgrims who do not wish to climb the mountain.

Below the pass on the other side of the mountain are the hospice and the church containing the rock which Roland, that most valiant hero, split from top to bottom with a triple stroke of his sword. Beyond this is Roncesvalles, scene of the great battle in which King Marsile[21], Roland, Oliver and forty thousand other warriors, both Christians and Saracens, were killed.

After this valley comes Navarre, which is well supplied with bread and wine, milk and livestock. The Navarrese and the Basques resemble one another in appearance, diet, dress and language; but the Basques have a fairer complexion than the Navarrese. The Navarrese wear short black garments reaching only to the knee, after the manner of the Scots. Their shoes, which they call *lavarcas*, are made of hairy untanned leather; they are tied on with thongs, and cover only the sole of the foot, leaving the upper part bare. They wear dark-coloured woollen cloaks, fringed like travelling

---

views—though hardly extending as far as the sea, some 40 miles away—from the crest road via Leizar-Athéka (see note 6).

21 Moslem king of Spain in the *Chanson de Roland*.

cloaks, which reach to the elbow and are known as *saias*. Coarsely dressed, they also eat and drink coarsely: in Navarre the whole household—master and servant, mistress and maid—eat from the same pot, in which all the food is mixed together, using their hands instead of spoons, and drink from the same cup. Watching them eat, you are reminded of dogs or pigs greedily gulping down their food; and when you hear them speaking it is like the barking of dogs. Their language is utterly barbarous: they call God *Urcia*, the Mother of God *Andrea Maria*, bread *orgui*, wine *ardum*, meat *aragui*, fish *araign*, a house *echea*, the master of the house *iaona*, the mistress *andrea*, a church *elicera*, the priest *belaterra* (which means 'good earth'), corn *gari*, water *uric*, the king *ereguia* and St James *Jaona domne Jacue*[22].

This is a barbarous people, different from all other peoples in customs and in race, malignant, dark in colour, ugly of face, debauched, perverse, faithless, dishonourable, corrupt, lustful, drunken, skilled in all forms of violence, fierce and savage, dishonest and false, impious and coarse, cruel and quarrelsome, incapable of any good impulses, past masters of all vices and iniquities. They resemble the Getae[23] and the Saracens in their malignance, and are in every way hostile to our French people. A Navarrese or a Basque

---

22 One of the earliest lists of Basque words, this has been described as the first mini-dictionary for travellers. Some of the words seem, however, to have been taken over from Latin or French: **domne** from 'dominus', **elicera** perhaps from 'ecclesia', **ereguia** from 'rex', **belaterra** possibly from French 'prêtre'.

23 The Getae, who lived round the mouth of the Danube in what is now Romania, were a byword in Roman times for cruelty and ferocity.

will kill a Frenchman for a penny if he can. In some parts of the region, in Biscay and Alava, when the Navarrese are warming themselves[24], men show their private parts to women and women to men. The Navarrese fornicate shamelessly with their beasts, and it is said that a Navarrese will put a padlock on his she-mule and his mare lest another man should get at them. He also libidinously kisses the vulva of a woman or a she-mule.

The Navarrese, therefore, are condemned by all right-minded people. But they are good in battle, though not in besieging fortresses[25]; and they are regular in the payment of tithes and accustomed to make offerings to the altar. Every day, when a Navarrese goes to church, he makes an offering to God of bread, wine, corn or some other substance. Wherever a Navarrese or Basque goes he has a horn round his neck like a hunter and carries two or three javelins, which he calls *auconas*. When he goes into his house or returns there he whistles like a kite; and when he is hiding in secret places or in some solitary spot with robbery in mind and wants to summon his companions without attracting notice he hoots like an owl or howls like a wolf.

---

24 A possible alternative translation is 'when the Navarrese become aroused'.
25 The translation here, following Vielliard and Herbers, reflects the contrast in the Latin text between *probi* (in battle) and *improbi* (in besieging fortresses). *Improbi* could, however, be taken as meaning 'vigorous' or 'energetic', suggesting that the Navarrese were good in both forms of conflict; this is the interpretation preferred by Bravo Lozano.

It is commonly said that the Basques are descended from the Scots; for they resemble them in customs and in appearance. Julius Caesar is said to have sent three peoples—the Nubians[26], the Scots and the tailed men of Cornwall[27]—into Spain to make war on the peoples of Spain who refused to pay him tribute, telling them to kill all males and to spare only the women. These peoples came to Spain by sea and after destroying their ships devastated the country by fire and sword, from Barcelona to Saragossa and from Bayonne to Mount Oca. They were unable to advance any farther, for the Castilians united and drove them out of their territory. In their flight they came to the coastal mountains between Nájera and Pamplona and Bayonne, on the seaward side in Biscay and Alava, where they settled down and built many fortresses. Having killed all the men, they took their wives by violence and had children by them, who later became known as Navarrese—the name being interpreted as *non verus* ('not true'), that is, not engendered of a pure race or legitimate stock. The Navarrese also used to derive their name from a town called Naddaver[28] in the country from which they originally came: a town which was converted to the

---

26 It has been suggested that the author of the 'Pilgrim's Guide' may have confused the Numiani, another tribe living in Britain, with the Nubians. But for further legendary support for the Nubian connection see note 28.
27 In medieval times the English were often credited with possessing tails.
28 Possibly the town of Nadabar in Ethiopia, where legend had it that Matthew preached the Gospel. This would tie in with the reference to the Nubians (above).

Lord in early times by the preaching of Matthew, the Apostle and Evangelist.

Leaving Navarre, the route runs through the forest of Oca and continues through Spanish territory—Castile and the Campos—in the direction of Burgos. This is a country full of treasures, of gold and silver, fortunate in producing fodder and sturdy horses and with an abundance of bread, wine, meat, fish, milk and honey. It is, however, lacking in trees, and the people are wicked and vicious.

Then, after crossing the territory of León and going over the passes of Monte Irago [Foncebadón] and Cebrero, you come into Galicia, a well wooded and well watered region with rivers and meadows and fine orchards, excellent fruit and clear springs, but with few towns and villages or cultivated fields. There is little wheaten bread or wine but ample supplies of rye bread and cider, cattle and horses, milk, honey and sea fish both large and small[29]. The country is rich in gold, silver, cloths, animal furs from the forests and other riches, as well as precious Saracen wares.

The Galicians are more like our French people in their customs than any other of the uncultivated races of Spain, but they have the reputation of being violent-tempered and quarrelsome.

---

[29] Alternatively, the sense may be that there are very large fish, but small numbers of them.

Chapter VIII

Of the Bodies of Saints which rest on the Road to St James and are to be visited by Pilgrims

Pilgrims going to St James by way of Saint-Gilles must in the first place pay honour to the body of the blessed Trophimus [Trophime][30] the Confessor in Arles. St Paul refers to him in his epistle to Timothy; he was consecrated as a bishop by Paul and sent by him to preach the Gospel in Arles for the first time. It was from this most clear spring, we are told by Pope Zosimus, that the whole of France received the waters of the faith. His feast is celebrated on 29th December.

Also to be visited in Arles is the body of the blessed Caesarius [Césaire][31], bishop and martyr, who instituted a Rule for nuns in that city. His feast is celebrated on 1st November.

---

30 Bishop of Arles in the 1st century, or according to another account in the 3rd; not the same as the Trophimus mentioned in 2 Timothy 4,20.
31 Archbishop of Arles in the 6th century. His feast-day is actually 27th August; 1st November is the feast-day of another St Caesarius.

In the cemetery of Arles pilgrims should seek out the relics of the blessed bishop Honoratus [Honorat][32], whose feast is celebrated on 16th January. In his venerable and magnificent basilica rests the body of the blessed Genesius [Genès][33], that most precious martyr. In the village of Trinquetaille near Arles, between two arms of the Rhône, is a magnificent tall marble column[34], standing behind the church of St Genesius, to which it is said he was tied by the faithless people before being beheaded; it is still stained red with his blood. Immediately after his execution the saint took his head and threw it into the Rhône; his body was carried down by the river to the basilica of St Honoratus, where it was given honourable burial. His head floated down the river to the sea and was conveyed under angelic guidance to Cartagena in Spain, where it now gloriously rests, performing numerous miracles. The saint's feast is celebrated on 25th August.

The pilgrim must then visit the cemetery near Arles known as Aliscamps and, as the custom is, intercede for the dead with prayers, psalms and alms. The cemetery is a mile long and a mile wide, and in no other cemetery can be found so many and such large marble tombs. They are of different forms and bear ancient inscriptions in Latin script but in unintelligible language. The farther

---

32 Bishop of Arles (d. 429); founder of the monastery of Lérins, to which his remains were transferred in 1392. His church in the Aliscamps cemetery (originally dedicated to St Genès) still survives.
33 Martyred at Arles in 303 or 308.
34 The column survived until the beginning of the 19th century, giving its name to the church of Saint-Genès de la Colonne.

you look the more sarcophagi you see. In this cemetery there are seven churches. If, in any one of them, a priest celebrates the Eucharist for the dead, or a layman has a mass said for them, or a clerk reads the psalter, they will be sure on the day of resurrection before God to find these pious dead helping them to obtain salvation; for many are the holy martyrs and confessors who rest here, and whose souls dwell amid the joys of Paradise. Their memory is celebrated, according to custom, on the Monday after the Easter octave.

A visit must also be paid, with a most attentive eye, to the venerable body of the blessed Aegidius [Gilles][35], the most pious confessor and abbot; for this most blessed saint, famed in all the countries of the world, must be venerated by all, worthily honoured by all and loved, invoked and supplicated by all. After the prophets and the apostles none among the blessed is worthier than he, none is more holy, none is more glorious, none is readier to help. It is he, more than any of the other saints, who comes most rapidly to the help of the needy and the afflicted and the suffering who call on his aid. What a fine and profitable act it is to visit his tomb! Anyone who prays to him with all his heart will assuredly be granted his help that very day. I have had personal experience of what I say: once in this saint's

---

35 St Gilles (Giles) was an 8th century hermit, founder of a monastery near the mouth of the Rhône, who became one of the most popular saints of the Middle Ages. Legend had it that he was born in Greece. The church of Saint-Gilles, 16 km west of Arles, preserves a fine Romanesque façade, but the saint's shrine, described below, is no longer in existence: it was apparently destroyed at some time between the 14th and 16th centuries.

town I saw a man who, on the very day that he had invoked this blessed confessor, escaped from an ancient house belonging to a cobbler named Peyrot just before it collapsed and was reduced to rubble. Who will spend most time at his place of burial? Who will worship God in his most holy basilica? Who will most frequently embrace his sarcophagus? Who will kiss his venerable altar or tell the story of his most pious life?

A sick man puts on the saint's tunic and is made well; a man bitten by a snake is cured by his inexhaustible virtue; another, possessed by a devil, is delivered; a storm at sea is quelled; the daughter of a man named Théocrite is restored to him after a long illness; a man sick in his whole body is restored to long-desired health; a hind, previously wild, is tamed by him and serves him; a community of monks flourishes under his rule as abbot; a demoniac is delivered from his demon; a sin committed by Charlemagne[36], revealed to him by an angel, is pardoned; a dead man is restored to life and a cripple to health; two doors of cypress-wood carved with images of the apostles are carried by the sea from Rome to the port on the Rhône, without anyone to direct them, solely by his sovereign power. I regret that my memory does not enable me to recount all his memorable deeds, so numerous and so great they are. This brilliant star from Greece, after illuminating the people of Provence with its rays, set magnificently among them, not declining but growing in size, not reducing its radiance but emitting it twice as strongly, not descending into the abyss but rising to the summits

---

[36] His incest with his sister Berthe, which resulted in the birth of Roland.

of Olympus. Its light did not die but became dark; and, made more brilliant than the other stars by its splendid satellites, it still illumines the four quarters of the world. The saint disappeared at midnight on the first day of September, a Sunday, and the choir of angels set him among them in a higher place, and the Gothic people, along with the community of monks, gave him honourable burial in their free territory, between the town of Nîmes and the Rhône.

A large golden shrine which is behind his altar and over his venerable body has on its left side, on the first level, the carved images of six apostles, and on the same level, in a leading place, is a finely carved image of the blessed Virgin Mary. On the second level, higher up, are the twelve signs of the zodiac, in the following order: the Ram, the Bull, the Twins, the Crab, the Lion, the Virgin, the Balance, the Scorpion, the Archer, the Goat, the Water-Bearer and the Fishes; and among them are golden flowers, twined like the tendrils of a vine. On the highest level (the third) are the images of twelve of the twenty-four elders[37], and above their heads are written these lines:

Here is the wondrous choir of the elders, twice twelve in number, who sing sweet songs on their clear-toned zithers.

On the right-hand side of the shrine, on the first level, there are, similarly, seven images, of whom six are apostles and the seventh is some disciple of Christ. Above the heads of the apostles, on both sides, are figures of the Virtues in the likeness of women:

---

[37] Revelation 4,4.

Goodness, Gentleness, Faith, Hope, Love and others. On the second level on the right-hand side are flowers in the form of a vine. On the highest level, as on the left-hand side, are images of twelve of the twenty-four elders, and above their heads are carved these lines:

This splendid shrine, decked with precious stones and gold, contains the remains of St Aegidius. May any man who damages it be eternally damned by the Lord and by St Aegidius and the whole heavenly host.

The roof of the shrine is decorated, on its upper surface and its sides, in the manner of fish scales. On its highest point are set thirteen pieces of rock crystal, some in the form of a chequerboard, others in the shape of apples or pomegranates. One large crystal is in the form of a great fish, a trout, with its tail turned upward. The first crystal, also very large, is in the shape of a jar, above which is a resplendent golden cross.

In the centre of the front of the shrine, in a circle of gold, is seated Our Lord, giving a blessing with His right hand and holding in His left[38] hand a book in which is written, 'Love ye peace and truth'. Under the stool on which His feet rest is a golden star, and round His shoulders, to right and left, are the letters A and Ω. And above His throne two precious stones glow with ineffable splendour. Round His throne are the four Evangelists, with wings, and under their feet are scrolls with the opening words of their gospels. On the right, above, is Matthew, in the form of a man, and below is Luke, in the form of an ox; and on the left, above, is

---

38 The Latin text, in error, repeats 'right'.

John, in the likeness of an eagle, and below is Mark, in the likeness of a lion. Beside the Lord's throne are two angels, marvellously carved: to the left a cherub, above Luke, and to the right a seraph, above Mark. Two rows of precious stones of all kinds, one round the Lord's throne and the other round the whole shrine, together with three stones set together to represent the divine Trinity, are of most splendid effect.

Some distinguished person, out of love for the most blessed confessor, has set his likeness in gold, fixed with golden nails, at the foot of the shrine, facing the altar, and it is still to be seen there today, for the glory of God. On the rear of the shrine is carved a representation of the Lord's Ascension. On the first level are six apostles, their eyes raised, watching the Lord entering into heaven, and above their heads are written these words: *Ye men of Galilee, why stand ye gazing up into heaven? This same Jesus, which is taken up from you into heaven, shall so come in like manner as ye have seen him go into heaven.*[39]

On the second level are six other apostles in the same posture, but there are golden columns between them. On the third level are the Lord, seated on a golden throne, and two angels, one on His right and one on His left, showing the Lord to the apostles, with one hand raised and the other bent down. And above the Lord's head, outside the throne, is a dove which appears to fly over Him. On the fourth level, the highest, the Lord is represented on another golden throne, surrounded by the four Evangelists: on the south side Luke in the likeness of an ox, below, and Matthew in the form of a man, above; and on the north side Mark in the

[39] Acts 1,11.

form of a lion, below, and John in the shape of an eagle, above. It is to be noted that the Lord in Majesty is not seated on His throne but is standing, with His back to the south and His eyes raised towards heaven. His right hand is raised, and in His left He holds a small cross. Thus He ascends to the Father, Who, on the highest point of the shrine, receives Him.

Such is the tomb of the blessed Aegidius, confessor, in which his venerable body rests with honour. May they blush with shame, those Hungarians[40] who claim to have his body; may they be dismayed, those monks of Chamalières[41] who think they have his whole body; may they be confounded, those men of Saint-Seine[42] who assert that they possess his head; may they be struck with fear, those Normans of Coutances[43] who boast that they have his whole body; for his most holy bones, as many have borne witness, could not be removed from his own town. Certain men once attempted by fraud to carry off the venerable arm of the blessed confessor to distant lands, but were quite unable to remove it.

There are four holy bodies which, it is said on the evidence of many witnesses, were never removed from their sarcophagi—those of the blessed James, son of

---

40 The Hungarians had a particular devotion to St Giles, and there was a monastery in Hungary dependent on the French abbey of Saint-Gilles.
41 The monastery of Chamalières, in the département of Haute-Loire, was dedicated to St Giles.
42 Probably Saint-Seine-l'Abbaye in the Côte-d'Or département, which had a church dedicated to St Giles.
43 The church of Saint-Gilles, in the diocese of Coutances, was believed at one time to have possessed the saint's body.

Zebedee, the blessed Martin of Tours, St Leonard of Limousin and the blessed Aegidius, confessor. It is reported that Philip[44], king of the French, once attempted to carry off these bodies to France[45] but was unable to remove them from their sarcophagi.

Those who go to St James by the Toulouse road must visit the body of the blessed confessor William[46]. This most holy William was a count and military leader in the service of Charlemagne, a valiant warrior, skilled in the art of war. We are told that by his courage and valour he won Nîmes, Orange and many other places for Christendom and brought wood from our Saviour's cross to the valley of Gellone, where he led the life of a hermit and where he now rests in honour after making a good end. His feast is celebrated on 28th May.

Also to be visited on the Toulouse road are the bodies of the blessed martyrs Tiberius [Thibéry], Modestus [Modeste] and Florence[47], who suffered a variety of torments and were martyred for the Christian faith in the time of Diocletian. They rest in a very handsome tomb on the banks of the Hérault; their feast is celebrated on 10th November.

---

44 Probably Philip I (1060–1108).
45 France (in the Latin text *Gallia*) here means the original core of the French kingdom, the Ile-de-France.
46 William (Guillaume) of Aquitaine, Count of Toulouse, fought against the Saracens under Charlemagne and later founded a monastery at Gellone (known after his death as Saint-Guilhem-le-Désert, département of Hérault), in which he became a monk. He features in the French *chansons de geste* as Guillaume d'Orange.
47 All martyred at Agde in 304 and buried in the abbey of Saint-Thibéry (département of Hérault).

On this road, too, and also to be visited is the most holy body of the blessed Saturninus [Sernin][48], bishop and martyr, who was first imprisoned by the pagans in the Capitol in Toulouse and then tied to wild and untamed bulls and dragged down the stone steps from the highest point of the Capitol for a distance of a mile. His head shattered, his brain beaten out, his whole body broken, he worthily rendered up his soul to Christ. He was buried in a most excellent place near the town of Toulouse, and a large basilica was built by the faithful in his honour. The Rule of the canons of St Augustine is observed there, and many benefits are granted by God to those who ask for them. The saint's feast is celebrated on 29th November.

Those Burgundians and Germans who go to St James by the Le Puy road should venerate the relics of the blessed Faith [Foy][49], virgin and martyr, whose soul, after her beheading on the hill in the town of Agen, was borne up to heaven in the form of a dove by choirs of angels and crowned with the laurels of immortality. When the blessed Caprasius [Caprais][50], bishop of Agen, heard this while hiding in a cave to escape the rage of persecution he found the courage to face

---

48 First bishop of Toulouse, martyred in 250. His remains are now housed in an 18th century tomb in the Basilique Saint-Sernin in Toulouse, France's largest and most complete surviving Romanesque church.

49 Sainte Foy d'Agen, martyred in 286–87. Her remains were stolen from Agen in the late 9th century and taken to Conques (département of Aveyron), where they are still preserved in the treasury of the church of Sainte-Foy. This pious theft is discreetly glossed over in the next paragraph.

50 The date of his martyrdom is given as 303.

martyrdom, hastened to the place where the blessed virgin had suffered and himself gained the palm of martyrdom, bearing himself most valiantly and even reproaching his executioners for their slowness.

Thereafter the most precious body of the blessed Faith, virgin and martyr, was honourably buried by Christians in the valley commonly known as Conques. Over her tomb was built a handsome basilica, in which the Rule of St Benedict is strictly observed to this day for the glory of God. Many benefits are granted both to the sick and to those who are in good health. In front of the basilica is a most excellent spring, the virtues of which are too great to be told. The saint's feast is celebrated on 6th October.

Then, on the road to St James by way of Saint-Léonard [de Noblat], the most holy body of the blessed Mary Magdalene is above all to be venerated[51]. This is that glorious Mary who in the house of Simon the Leper watered the Saviour's feet with her tears, wiped them with her hair, kissed them and anointed them with a precious ointment. Accordingly her many sins were forgiven her, for she had greatly loved Jesus Christ her Redeemer, Who loves all men. It was she who after the Lord's Ascension left Jerusalem with the blessed Maximinus and other disciples of the Lord, sailed to Provence and landed at the port of Marseilles. She lived the life of a hermit in that country for some years and was then buried in Aix by Maximinus, who had become bishop of the town. Much later a sanctified monk named Badilo translated her most precious relics to Vézelay, where they now rest in an honourable tomb.

---

51 At Vézelay (département of Yonne).

There a large and beautiful basilica and an abbey were built; there sinners have their faults remitted by God for love of the saint, the blind have their sight restored, the tongues of the dumb are loosed, the lame are cured of their lameness, those possessed by devils are delivered and ineffable benefits are granted to many of the faithful. The saint's feast is celebrated on 22nd July.

Also to be visited is the sacred body of the blessed Leonard the confessor. The scion of a noble Frankish family, brought up at the royal court, he renounced the vicious life of the world for love of the supreme God and for many years led the life of a hermit at Noblat[52] in Limousin, frequently fasting and spending many nights in vigils, in cold and nakedness and unspeakable sufferings. After a good death he was laid to rest on his own land, and his sacred remains have since remained there. May they blush with shame, therefore, those monks of Corbigny[53] who claim to possess his body; for, as we have said, not the least of his bones nor any of his dust can be moved from their resting place. The monks of Corbigny, like many other people, have benefited from his works and his miracles; but they are without his corporeal presence. Since they cannot have his body they venerate, as being his, the body of one Léotard, which they say was brought to them from Anjou in a silver shrine. They have changed his name after his death, as if in a second baptism, and have given him the

---

52 Now called Saint-Léonard de Noblat (département of Haute-Vienne).

53 In the département of Nièvre. The St Léonard venerated at Corbigny—who seems always to have been known by that name—was a different saint.

name of St Leonard so that pilgrims may be attracted by such a great and famous name and may enrich them with their offerings. They celebrate his feast on 15th October. First they made St Leonard of Limousin patron of their church; then they put another man in his place, like envious serfs who seize their master's inheritance by violence and give it improperly to another. They are like a wicked father who takes his daughter away from her rightful husband and gives her to another man. In the words of the Psalmist, *they have changed their glory into the similitude of an ox.*[54] A wise man rebukes those who do such deeds, saying, 'Do not give thine honour unto others.'[55] Both strangers and local people go to Corbigny thinking to find there the body of St Leonard of Limousin which they love and, without knowing it, find another in its place. Whoever it is that performs miracles at Corbigny, it is the blessed Leonard of Limousin who delivers captives and brings pilgrims to the shrine, even though he has been supplanted as patron of the church. Thus the men of Corbigny are guilty of a double fault, since they do not recognise him who generously enriches them with his miracles and do not even celebrate his feast, but, in their disorder, do honour to another in his place.

The divine clemency has thus diffused the glory of the blessed confessor Leonard of Limousin far and wide throughout the whole world, and his powerful intercession has released countless thousands of captives from prison; and their iron chains, more barbarous than can be described, hang in thousands all

---
54 Psalm 106,20.
55 Proverbs 5,9.

round his church, to right and left, inside and outside, in witness to such great miracles. When you see the columns laden with so many heavy and barbarous chains you will be more astonished than words can tell. There you will see hanging iron handcuffs, collars, chains, fetters, and a variety of other devices, traps, padlocks, yokes, helmets, scythes and other instruments from which this potent confessor has freed captives by his mighty power[56]. What is remarkable about him is that he is accustomed to appear in visible human form to those confined in prisons, even beyond the sea, as those whom he has liberated by divine power will bear witness. In him is fulfilled what the divine prophet proclaimed, saying, *'Many times he liberated such as sit in darkness and in the shadow of death, bound in affliction and iron. And they cried to him in their trouble, and he saved them out of their distresses. For he brought them out of their iniquities, breaking the gates of brass and cutting the bars of iron in sunder; and he liberated men bound with chains and many nobles in fetters of iron.'*[57] Many times, indeed, Christians were handed over in chains to the Gentiles, like Bohemond[58], and made slaves to those who hated them, and suffered tribulations at the hands of their enemies and were humiliated by them. The saint said to those who were in chains, *'Go forth'*, and to those who

---

56 The church of Saint-Léonard-de-Noblat still displays a symbolic length of chain.

57 Based on Psalm 107, verses 10, 13, 16 and 17 and Psalm 149, verse 8.

58 Bohemond, Prince of Antioch, who took part in the first Crusade and was captured by the Moslems and held in prison for three years.

were in darkness, *'Shew yourselves'*[59]. His feast is celebrated on 6th November.

After St Leonard a visit must be paid in the town of Périgueux to the body of the blessed Fronto [Front][60], bishop and confessor, who was consecrated as a bishop by the Apostle Peter in Rome and was sent to preach in Périgueux along with a priest named George. They set out together, but George died on the way: whereupon, after his burial, the blessed Fronto returned to the Apostle and told him of the death of his companion. St Peter gave him his staff, saying, 'Go, set this staff of mine over the body of your companion and say, "In virtue of the mission you received from the Apostle, rise up in the name of Christ and accomplish it."' And he did so, and thanks to the Apostle's staff the blessed Fronto recovered his companion from death, and went on to convert the city by his preaching. He performed numerous miracles, and after a worthy death was buried in the basilica which had been built in his name. In this church, by the grace of God, many benefits are granted to those who ask for them. It is said by some that he was a member of the college of Christ's disciples. His tomb[61] is like the tomb of no other saint, having been most carefully built in the form of a rotunda like the Holy Sepulchre, and it surpasses in the beauty of its workmanship the tombs of all other saints. His feast is celebrated on 25th October.

---

59 Isaiah 49,9.
60 According to his legend, the first bishop of Périgueux. Legend also makes his companion George the first bishop of Le Puy.
61 In the Cathedral of Saint-Front, Périgueux; destroyed during the 16th century wars of religion.

Pilgrims who go to St James by the Tours road should see in Orléans the wood of the True Cross and the chalice of the blessed Evurtius [Euverte][62], bishop and confessor, in the church of the Holy Cross. One day when St Evurtius was saying mass the hand of God in human form appeared in the air above the altar so that all present could see it. All that the bishop did at the altar the hand did also: when he made the sign of the cross over the bread and the chalice the hand did the same, and when he elevated the bread and the chalice the hand of God also raised bread and a chalice. After the sacrifice of the mass was completed the most sacred hand of the Saviour disappeared. Thus we are led to understand that whenever a priest sings mass Christ sings it also. Hence the words of the blessed doctor Fulgentius[63]: 'It is not man who offers the sacrifice of the body and blood of Christ, but Christ Himself, Who was crucified for us.' And the blessed Isidore[64] says: 'The sacrifice is no better on account of the goodness of a good priest, and no worse on account of the badness of a bad one.' The chalice is always held ready in the church of the Holy Cross for those, whether local people or strangers, who wish to take communion.

---

62 A 4th century bishop of Orléans who was credited with the foundation of a church to house a relic of the Cross. The present cathedral of Sainte-Croix is the third church on the site.

63 Either Fulgentius, bishop of Ruspe in Africa (467–532), a prominent theologian in his day, or St Fulgentius, bishop of Ecija in Andalusia (d. c. 633), brother of St Isidore of Seville.

64 St Isidore of Seville (c. 560–636), the great encyclopaedic writer. Originally buried in Seville, his remains were transferred to León in the 11th century.

Pilgrims should also venerate in Orléans the body of the blessed Evurtius, bishop and confessor, and, in the church of Saint-Samson, the paten which was actually used in the Last Supper[65].

Pilgrims travelling on this road should also pay honour, on the banks of the Loire, to the venerable body of the blessed Martin[66], bishop and confessor, who gloriously brought three dead men back to life and is reported to have restored lepers, men possessed by devils, the sick, the lunatic and the demoniac, and sufferers from other diseases, to the health they desired. The shrine containing his most sacred remains, in the city of Tours, is resplendent with a profusion of gold, silver and precious stones and is graced by numerous miracles. Over it a great and splendid basilica[67], in the likeness of the church of St James, has been built. The sick come to it and are made well, the possessed are delivered, the blind see, the lame stand upright, all kinds of sickness are cured and all those who ask for the saint's intercession are fully satisfied. His glorious renown, therefore, is spread throughout the world in well merited eulogies, for the honour of Christ. His feast is celebrated on 11th November.

---

65 The present church of Saint-Euverte, on the east side of Orléans, was built in the late 12th century and rebuilt in the 15th. The church of Saint-Samson and Saint-Symphorien, belonging to the priory of Saint-Martin-des-Champs, was founded in 1067.
66 The great 4th century bishop of Tours who became one of the most popular French saints.
67 Demolished in 1802.

Then in the town of Poitiers the most holy remains of Hilary [Hilaire][68], bishop and confessor, must be visited. Among other miracles this saint, filled with divine grace, defeated the Arian heresy and maintained the unity of the faith. But Leo, the heretic, refused to accept his sacred writings, left the Council and died shamefully when his entrails burst in the latrines. When, during the Council, Hilary desired to sit down the ground rose miraculously to provide him with a seat. By the sound of his voice alone he was able to break the locks on the doors of the council chamber. Exiled for his Catholic faith, he spent four years on an island in Phrygia, and while there drove out innumerable snakes by the force of his authority. In Poitiers he restored to a weeping mother a child which had died a double death[69]. The tomb in which he rests is decorated with a profusion of gold, silver and precious stones, and his large and beautiful basilica is graced by frequent miracles. His feast is celebrated on 13th January.

Also to be visited is the venerable head of the blessed John the Baptist, which was brought by certain religious men from Jerusalem to a place called Angély[70]

[68] Bishop of Poitiers in the 4th century. The church of Saint-Hilaire-le-Grand, with the saint's shrine, still survives. Hilary was a determined opponent of the Arian heresy (which asserted that Christ was not of one substance with the Father) and was exiled to Phrygia by the Arian Emperor Constantius, but the rest of the legend recorded in this paragraph is confused; Leo the heretic cannot be identified.

[69] A double death because the child, dying unbaptised, lost the life of the soul as well as the life of the body.

[70] Now called Saint-Jean-d'Angély (département of Charente-Maritime). Nothing remains of the saint's basilica.

in Poitou. There a great and magnificent basilica was built and dedicated to him, and in this his most sacred head is venerated night and day by a choir of a hundred monks and has wrought countless miracles. While the head was being transported by sea and by land it gave many proofs of its miraculous power: on the sea it warded off numerous perils, and on land it brought dead men back to life. Accordingly it is believed to be indeed the head of the venerable Forerunner. It was found on 24th February in the time of the Emperor Marcian, when the Forerunner first revealed to two monks the place where his head was concealed.

At Saintes, on the road to St James, pilgrims must pay due honour to the body of the blessed Eutropius [Eutrope][71], bishop and martyr. His most sacred passion was written in Greek by his companion Dionysius [Denis], bishop of Paris, and sent by the hand of the blessed Pope Clement to his parents in Greece, who already believed in Christ. I found this Passion in the Greek school in Constantinople, in a book containing

---

71 Held to be the first bishop of Saintes; but there is much confusion about his date. The *Acta Sanctorum* assign him to the 1st century, which seems improbably early. His association with St Denis (Dionysius), first bishop of Paris, would put him in the 3rd century. But this Dionysius became confused in early medieval times with Dionysius the Areopagite, baptised in Athens by Paul, making the connection with the 1st century Pope Clement I more plausible. The letter from Dionysius to Clement (in which he describes himself as 'bishop of the Franks' and also refers to his baptism by Paul) is evidently apocryphal.

The saint's sarcophagus, rediscovered and restored in the 19th century, is preserved in the church of Saint-Eutrope in Saintes.

the passions of several holy martyrs, and, for the glory of our Lord Jesus Christ and His glorious martyr Eutropius, have translated it from Greek into Latin to the best of my ability. It began thus:

Dionysius, bishop of the Franks, a Greek by race, to the most reverend Pope Clement, greetings in Christ. We have to inform you that Eutropius, whom you sent with me into these regions to preach the name of Christ, has received the crown of martyrdom at the hands of the gentiles in the town of Saintes for the faith of the Lord. Accordingly I humbly beseech Your Paternity not to delay in sending this book of his passion as quickly as possible to my relatives, acquaintances and faithful friends in Greece, particularly in Athens, so that they and the others who, with me, received from the blessed Paul the baptism of a new regeneration may, on hearing that this glorious martyr has met a cruel death for the faith of Christ, rejoice at suffering tribulations and torments in Christ's name. And if by chance the fury of the gentiles should inflict some form of martyrdom on them may they learn to suffer it patiently for Christ's sake and have no fear of it. For all those who desire to live piously in Christ must bear the infamies of the impious and the heretics and despise them as mad and foolish, since we must pass through many tribulations to enter into the kingdom of God.

And now, far from you in body but close in desire and in spirit, I say farewell for eternity[72].

* * * * *

---

72 This concluding sentence is in four lines of rhyming Latin verse.

Here begins the Passion of the blessed Eutropius of Saintes, Bishop and Martyr

Eutropius, the most glorious martyr of Christ, the goodly bishop of Saintes, scion of a noble family of Persia, was descended from the most excellent stock in all the world, having been begotten by a Babylonian emir named Xerses on Queen Guiva. After his conversion none could be of more noble rank, none of greater humility, in both faith and works.

While still a boy he studied the writings of the Chaldaeans and the Greeks, and showed himself the equal of the greatest persons of the kingdom in wisdom and desire for knowledge; then he went to the court of King Herod in Galilee, wishing to discover whether there was anything new or of interest to be found there. After some days at the court, hearing of the miracles wrought by the Saviour, he sought Him from place to place; and, since He had gone to the other side of the Sea of Galilee, which is called Tiberias, with the great crowds of people who followed Him and observed the wonders He was performing, Eutropius too followed Him.

Then one day, by divine grace, the Saviour in His ineffable generosity satisfied the hunger of the five thousand people who were with Him with five loaves and two fishes. Seeing this miracle, the young Eutropius, who had already heard about His other miracles and already believed a little in Him, desired to speak to Him but did not dare, being afraid of a reprimand from Nicanor, the tutor to whom his father had entrusted him. Nourished by the bread of divine grace, however, he went to Jerusalem and after worshipping the Creator in the temple, after the manner of the gentiles, returned to his father's house. There he told his father all that he had observed with such attention in the country from which he had come. 'I have seen,' he said, 'a man who is called Christ and who has not his like in the whole world. He brings the dead back to life, purifies lepers, restores sight to the blind and hearing to the deaf, gives strength to cripples and health to all who are sick. What more can I say? I saw him feeding five thousand people on five loaves and two fishes, and with what was left over his disciples filled twelve baskets. Where he is there is no hunger, no foul weather, no death. If the creator of heaven and earth ever deigns to send him to our country I beg you, of your grace, to do him honour.'

After hearing this, and much else to the same intent, the emir considered within himself how he might see this man. Soon afterwards, having obtained his father's permission, the boy, desiring to see the Lord again, went to Jerusalem to worship in the temple. With him were Warradac, commander of the king's armies, Nicanor, the royal seneschal and the boy's tutor, and many other nobles whom the king sent with him for his protection. One day, on his way back from the temple, he saw the Lord returning from Bethany, where He had brought Lazarus back to life. A great crowd of people were flocking through the gates of Jerusalem to meet Him; and, seeing the children of the Jews and the multitude of people of other nations going towards

Him, strewing flowers and branches of palms, olives and other trees in His path and crying 'Hosanna to the Son of David', Eutropius felt unspeakable joy and began likewise to strew flowers in His path. Then people told him that He had brought Lazarus back to life after he had been dead for four days; and, hearing this, he rejoiced greatly. But since on account of the multitude of people he could not see the Saviour properly he was much saddened; for he was with those people of whom John speaks in his gospel: *'And there were certain Greeks among them that came up to worship at the feast. The same came therefore to Philip, which was of Bethsaida of Galilee, and desired him, saying, Sir, we would see Jesus.'*[73] Then Philip, along with Andrew, told the Lord, and at once the blessed Eutropius, with his companions, saw Him face to face and, rejoicing greatly, began secretly to believe in Him. Finally he became wholly attached to Him, but was afraid of the opinions of his companions, who had been strictly enjoined by his father to watch over him carefully and bring him home.

Then certain people told him that the Jews were about to kill the Lord; and since he did not wish to witness the death of such a man he left Jerusalem on the following day. Returning to his father, he related in due order to all in his country all that he had seen concerning the Saviour in Jerusalem. Then, after a brief stay in Babylon, since he desired to attach himself wholly to the Saviour and believed that He was still alive in the body, he went back to Jerusalem along with a squire, unknown to his father, forty-five days later. He soon sorrowed to hear that the Lord Whom he loved in

---
[73] John 12,20–21.

secret had suffered on the cross and been killed by the Jews; but when he learned that He had risen from the dead and appeared to His disciples and ascended into heaven in triumph he began to rejoice greatly.

Then on the day of Pentecost he was with the Lord's disciples and was told by them that the Holy Ghost had descended on them in the form of tongues of fire and had filled their hearts and taught them the languages of all peoples. And so, filled with the Holy Ghost, he returned to Babylon and, burning with the love of Christ, put to the sword the Jews whom he encountered in that country because they had brought shame on Jerusalem by killing the Lord.

Soon afterwards, when the Lord's disciples were travelling to the various countries in the world, two golden luminaries of the faith, Simon and Thaddaeus, apostles of the Lord, were sent to Persia by the action of divine grace. And when they came to Babylon, after expelling from the country the magi Zaroen and Arfaxat, who were turning people away from the faith by their vain conceits and marvels, these apostles distributed to all the seeds of eternal life and performed miracles of all kinds.

Then the blessed youth Eutropius, rejoiced by their coming, called on the king to depart from the error of the gentiles and their idols and submit to the Christian faith, by which he would earn the kingdom of heaven. What need I say more? At once, after hearing the preaching of the apostles, the king and his son, together with many citizens of Babylon, were regenerated by the grace of baptism, which they received at the apostles' hands.

Finally, when the whole city had been converted to the faith of the Lord, the apostles founded a church there with all the orders of clergy. They appointed the most faithful Abdias, a man imbued with evangelical doctrine whom they had brought with them from Jerusalem, to be bishop over the Christian people, and ordained Eutropius as archdeacon. Then they set out for other cities, preaching the word of God. And when, not many days after, they ended their life on earth with the triumph of martyrdom, the blessed Eutropius celebrated their passion in Chaldaean and Greek. Then, hearing of the miracles and the virtues of the blessed Peter, prince of the apostles, who then held the apostolic office in Rome, he renounced altogether the life of the world and, with the permission of his bishop but without the knowledge of his father, made his way to Rome. There he was benevolently received by the blessed Peter and imbued by him with the Lord's precepts.

After staying for some time with Peter he departed, by his order and with his counsel, to preach in France along with other brethren. And when he came to the town called Saintes and found it well enclosed on all sides by ancient walls, decked with tall towers, magnificently situated, fairly proportioned in both length and breadth, abounding in all delights and all provisions, replete with fair meadows and clear fountains, traversed by a great river, richly girdled by gardens and orchards and vineyards, with a salubrious air, pleasant squares and streets—indeed delightful in every respect—this zealous apostle began to think that God would find this most fair and excellent city worthy to be converted from the error of the gentiles and the worship of idols and brought to acknowledge the laws of Christianity. And so he went about the squares and streets of the city ardently preaching the word of God. But soon, when the people realised that he was a stranger and heard him speaking of the Holy Trinity and of baptism, words previously unknown to them, they were filled with wrath and drove him out of the city, after burning him with torches and cruelly beating him with cudgels. He bore this persecution patiently and built a wooden hut on a hill near the city, where he lived for many months, preaching in the city during the day and spending the night in his hut in vigils, prayers and tears.

After a long period, having failed to convert more than a few to Christ by his preaching, he remembered the Lord's precept: *And whosoever shall not receive you, nor hear your words, when ye depart out of that house or city, shake off the dust of your feet.*[74] Then he returned to Rome, where the blessed Peter had suffered martyrdom on the cross, and was enjoined by St Clement, who was then Pope, to go back to the above-mentioned city, preach the Lord's precepts and await the crown of martyrdom. And so, having been consecrated as a bishop by the Pope himself, he set off with the blessed Dionysius [Denis], who had come to Rome from Greece, and with other brethren whom Clement sent to preach in France, and came to Auxerre. There they separated, with embraces of divine love and tearful farewells, and Dionysius and his companions made for Paris, while the blessed Eutropius returned to Saintes, ready to suffer

---

74 Matthew 10,14

martyrdom bravely. Filled with zeal for Christ, he fortified himself with these words: *The Lord is on my side: I will not fear: what can man do unto me?... And fear not them which kill the body, but are not able to kill the soul... Skin for skin, yea, all that a man hath will he give for his life.*[75]

Then he went into the city with a firm step and, like one struck mad, preached the faith of the Lord in season and out of season, teaching to all men the incarnation of Christ, His Passion, His Resurrection, His Ascension and all He suffered for the salvation of mankind, and proclaiming publicly to all that no man can enter into God's kingdom unless he has been reborn by water and the Holy Ghost. At night he lived in his hut as he had done before; and as he preached, with divine grace coming down from above, many gentiles were baptised by him in the city. Among those regenerated by the water of baptism was a daughter of the king of the city, Eustella by name. When her father heard this he cursed her and drove her out of the city; and she, seeing that she was driven out for the love of Christ, took up her dwelling near the holy man's hut. Then her father, moved by love for his daughter, sent messengers to her again and again, asking her to return home; but she replied that she would rather live outside the city for the faith of Christ than return to it and be defiled by idols. Filled with anger, her father called together all the butchers in the city, a hundred and fifty in number, and ordered them to kill St Eutropius and bring the girl back to his house. And on 30th April the butchers,

---

[75] Psalm 118,6; Matthew 10,28; Job 2,4.

accompanied by a multitude of gentiles, went to the above-mentioned hut and began by stoning the most blessed man of God; then they struck his naked body with cudgels and leaded ropes; and finally they killed him by beheading him with axes and hatchets.

The maiden, with the help of a number of Christians, buried him at night in his hut, and so long as she lived maintained a perpetual vigil over his grave, with candles and divine services. And when she left this world, dying a holy death, she asked to be buried near the tomb of her master, on land which had belonged to him.

Later a great and magnificently built church was erected by the faithful over the most holy body of the blessed Eutropius, in his honour and in the name of the holy and indivisible Trinity. Those who come to it afflicted with all kinds of diseases are quickly cured, the crippled are made straight, the blind are given sight, the deaf recover hearing, those possessed of a devil are delivered and salutary aid is given to all those who ask for it with a sincere heart. Hanging in the church are iron chains and handcuffs and other iron instruments of different kinds struck off prisoners by the blessed Eutropius. May he, by his great merits and his prayers, obtain pardon for us from God, wipe out our sins, revive the virtues within us, direct our lives, rescue us in the dangerous hour of death from the jaws of hell, appease for us the wrath of the eternal Judge on the last day and lead us into the kingdom of heaven, with the aid of our Lord Jesus Christ, Who with the Father and the Holy Ghost reigns as God, from eternity to eternity.

Amen.

* * * * *

Then at Blaye, on the coast, pilgrims must ask for the aid of the blessed Romanus [Romain][76], in whose basilica rests the body of the blessed Roland, martyr. The scion of a noble family, a count in the service of Charlemagne and one of his twelve companions in arms, he entered Spain, moved by zeal for the faith, to expel the infidels. His strength was such that at Roncesvalles, it is said, he clove a rock from top to bottom with three strokes of his sword. It is also said that in blowing his horn he blew with such force that he split it in two. This ivory horn is in the basilica of Saint-Seurin in Bordeaux. Over the rock of Roncesvalles a church was built. After defeating kings and peoples in many wars, Roland, that valiant martyr for Christ—exhausted by hunger, cold and excessive heat, having suffered violent blows and many scourgings for the love of God and been pierced by arrows and lances—is said to have died of thirst in the valley of Roncesvalles. His most blessed body was given respectful burial by his companions in the basilica of Saint-Romain in Blaye.

Then at Bordeaux a visit must be paid to the body of the blessed Severinus [Seurin][77], bishop and confessor. His feast is celebrated on 23rd October.

In the village of Belin, in the Landes of Bordeaux, pilgrims should pay honour to the bodies of the holy martyrs Oliver, Gondebaud king of Friesland, Ogier king of Denmark, Arastain king of Brittany, Garin duke of Lorraine and many other companions in arms of Charlemagne who, after conquering the pagan armies,

---
76 A disciple of St Martin of Tours (4th century).
77 Bishop of Bordeaux in the 5th century.

55

were killed in Spain for the Christian faith[78]. Their companions brought their precious bodies back to Belin and buried them with great reverence. They lie all together in the same tomb, and from the tomb emanates a sweet perfume which heals the sick.

Then in Spain[79] pilgrims should visit the body of the blessed Dominic[80], the confessor, who made the paved road between the town of Nájera and Redecilla, on which he now rests.

Also to be visited are the bodies of the blessed martyrs Facundus and Primitivus, whose basilica was built by Charlemagne. At their town[81] is a meadow planted with trees in which, it is said, the lances of the warriors, set in the ground, put on leaves. Their feast is celebrated on 27th November.

---

78 All these legendary martyrs are heroes of the French medieval epics.
79 The strong French sympathies of the author of the 'Guide' evident in earlier chapters is again reflected in the many pages devoted to French saints and shrines compared with the brief treatment of shrines in Spain.
80 Santo Domingo de la Calzada. His tomb is now in the town of that name.
81 Sahagún. The town features in the legend of Charlemagne's expedition into Spain as the scene of a great victory over the Moors. The legend has it that on the night before the battle the Frankish knights set their lances into the ground on the banks of the Río Cea, just outside the town. Some of the lances miraculously took root during the night and put out leaves; and it turned out on the following day that these were the lances of the knights who died in the battle and who had thus received by anticipation the palms of martyrdom. The poplars now growing on the banks of the river are said to be descended from the flowering lances.

Then in the town of León pilgrims should go to see the venerable body of the blessed Isidore[82], bishop, confessor and doctor, who instituted a most pious rule for clerks, imbued the Spanish people with his teachings and adorned the whole of Holy Church with his fruitful writings.

Finally and above all pilgrims are to visit and pay the greatest veneration to the most holy body of the blessed apostle James in the city of Compostella.

May the saints mentioned here and all the other saints of God intercede for us, through their merits and their prayers, with Our Lord Jesus Christ, Who lives and reigns with the Father and the Holy Ghost, God from eternity to eternity.

Amen.

---

82 St Isidore of Seville (cf. note 64). In 1063 his remains were transferred from Moslem-occupied Seville to the church of San Isidoro in León, built by Fernando I of Castile and León to receive them.

Chapter IX

Of the Characteristics of the City and the Basilica of the Apostle St James in Galicia

Pope Callistus and Aimery, the Chancellor

The city of Compostella lies between two rivers, the Sar to the east, between the Monte del Gozo and the city, and the Sarela to the west. The city has seven entrances and gates: the first is called the Porta Francigena[83], the second the Porta Penne[84], the third the Porta de Subfratribus[85], the fourth the Porta de Sancto Peregrino[86], the fifth the Porta de Falgueriis[87], which leads to Padrón, the sixth the Porta de Susannis[88] and

---

83 The French Gate: now the Puerta del Camino, on the north-east of the town. (All the gates except the Puerta de Mazarelos have disappeared, and the modern names refer only to their sites).
84 Now the Puerta de la Peña, on the north side.
85 The 'Gate below the Friars' (probably referring to the old hospice outside the north gate of the Cathedral); now the Puerta de San Martín (after the monastery of San Martín), on the north side of the town.
86 The Gate of the Holy Pilgrim; now the Puerta de la Trinidad (after the church of the Trinidad), on the west side.
87 Now the Puerta Fajera, on the south-west side.
88 Now the Puerta de Mámoa, on the south-east side.

59

Index to the Plan of the old City

A	Puerta del Camino	E	Puerta de la Trinidad
B	Puerta de San Roque	F	Puerta Fajera
C	Puerta de la Peña	G	Puerta de Mazarelos
D	Puerta de San Martín	H	Puerta de la Mámoa

1. Igl. de San Felix
2. Hospital Viejo
3. Hospital de la Calle de las Carnicerías Viejas
4. Monasterio de San Payo
5. Hospital de Jerusalén
6. Hospital de la Calle de Santa Cristina
7. Hospital fundado por Sarracino González
8. Hospital de N.S. del Camino
9. Hospital de Santa Ana
10. Hospital de la Reina
11. Hospital de Salomé
12. Hospital de San Juan
13. Hospital de San Roque
14. Hospital de Carretas
15. Hospital Real
16. Catedral
17. San Martín Pinario
18. Monasterio de San Pelayo
19. Colegio de San Jerónimo
20. Colegio de N.S. de los Remedios
21. Universidad
22. Convento de N.S. de la Cerca
23. Convento de la Enseñanza
24. Convento de las Mercedarias
25. Igl. de San Miguel dos Agros
26. Igl. de la Trinidad
27. Plaza de Cervantes
28. Travesía de Salomé
29. Convento de San Francisco
30. Cuesta de Anteltares
31. Capilla de las Animas
32. Rua y Plaza de la Algara de Abajo
33. Hospital de San Andrés
34. Calle de las Huertas

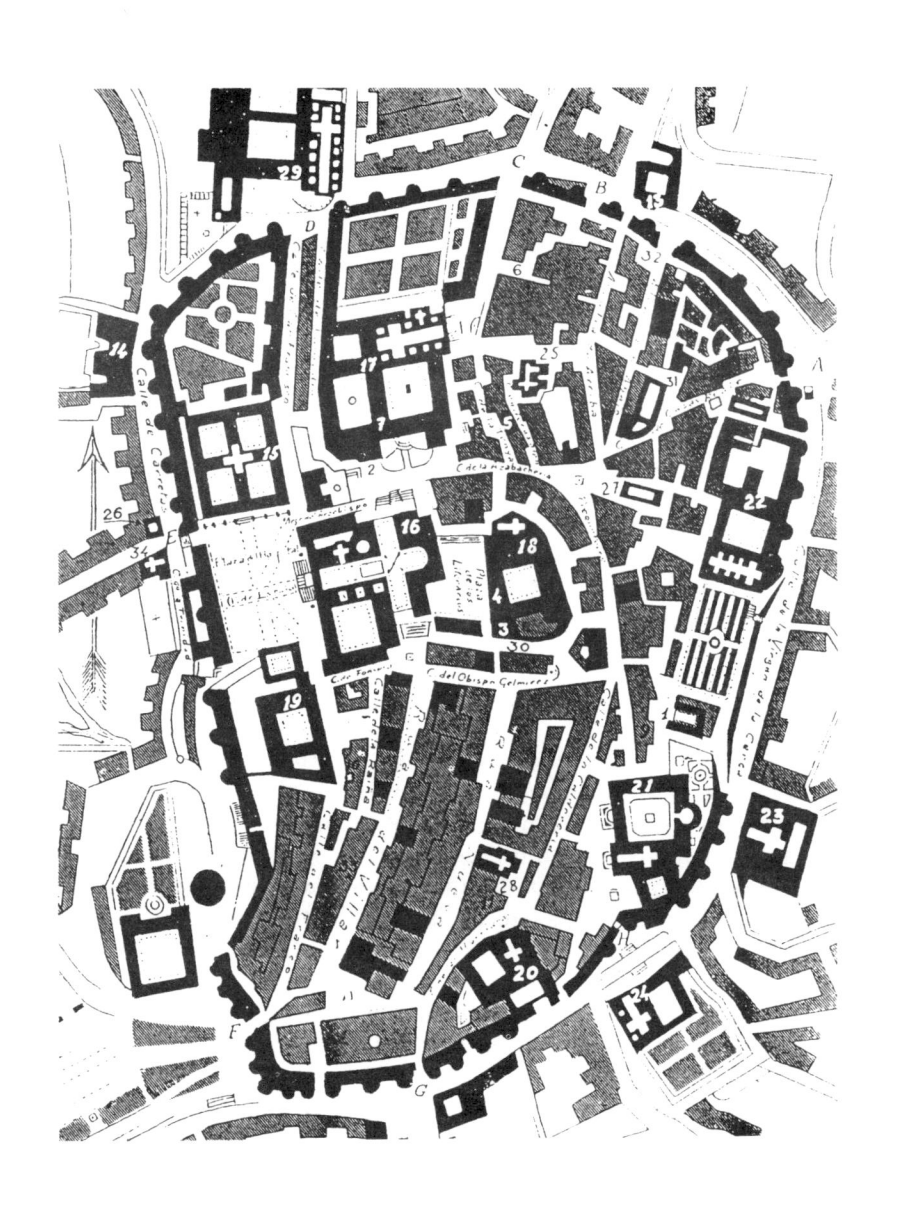

Plan of the old city.

the seventh the Porta de Macerellis[89], where the precious liquor of Bacchus enters the city.

Of the city's churches

In this city there are ten churches, the first of which is the church of the most glorious apostle James son of Zebedee, situated in the centre of the city, which is resplendent in glory. The second, dedicated to the blessed Apostle Peter, is an abbey of monks situated on the French Road[90]. The third is the church of St Michael of the Cistern[91]. The fourth is the church of St Martin of the Pinewood[92]. The fifth, Holy Trinity[93], is the burial-place for pilgrims. The sixth, dedicated to the virgin St Susanna[94], is on the road to Padrón. The seventh is dedicated to St Felix the martyr[95], the eighth to St

---

89 Now the Puerta de Mazarelos, on the south side. This is the only one of the old town gates to survive as a structure.
90 San Pedro d'Afora, which lay outside the walls on the Camino Francés; demolished in the 19th century.
91 San Miguel dos Agros. One of the earliest churches in Santiago, it was destroyed at the end of the 10th century, rebuilt in the early 12th century and almost entirely rebuilt in neo-classical style in the late 18th century.
92 San Martín Pinario, originally founded in the 9th century. The present magnificent buildings date from the 16th and 17th centuries.
93 A chapel near the Puerta de la Trinidad; demolished around 1930.
94 In the Paseo de la Herradura. Originally dedicated to the Santo Sepulcro, it was renamed when the relics of Santa Susana were brought here from Braga in 1102. The present church is 16th century.
95 San Félix (Fiz) de Solovio, the city's oldest surviving church,

Benedict[96]. The ninth, behind the basilica of St James, is dedicated to the martyr St Pelagius[97]. The tenth, dedicated to the Virgin Mary[98], is also behind the basilica of St James, and has an entrance to it between the altars of St Nicholas and the Holy Cross.

Of the dimensions of the church

The basilica of St James measures from end to end, that is from the west doorway to the altar of the Saviour[99], fifty-three times the height of a man; from side to side, that is from the French Doorway[100] to the south doorway, it measures thirty-nine times the height of a man; and its internal height is fourteen times the

---

originally the hermitage of Pelayo, who saw the star over the site of the Apostle's tomb. In its present form it dates from the early 12th century.
96 San Benito del Campo. Founded in the 10th century, it was rebuilt in the 12th century and again in the 18th century in its present neo-classical style.
97 San Pelayo de Antealtares. The monastery, situated close to the Cathedral 'in front of the altars', was founded in the 9th century to house the monks looking after the newly discovered tomb of the Apostle. Originally dedicated to St Peter, it was rededicated to San Pelayo in 1152. The present buildings date mostly from the 17th and 18th centuries.
98 Now part of the Cathedral as the chapel of Santa María de Corticela.
99 The Capilla de San Salvador, now also known as the Capilla del Rey de Francia because it was endowed by Charles V of France in the 14th century, is the central apsidal chapel at the east end of the Cathedral.
100 The Porta Francigena, the north doorway.

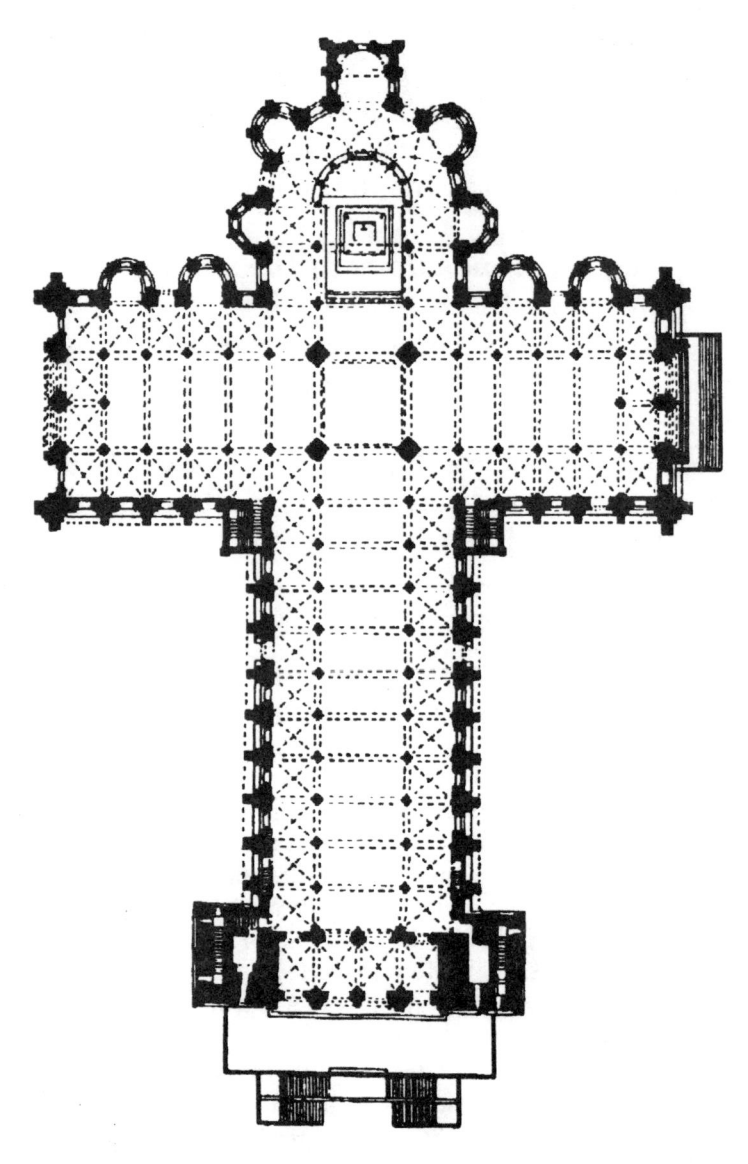

Plan of the Romanesque Cathedral

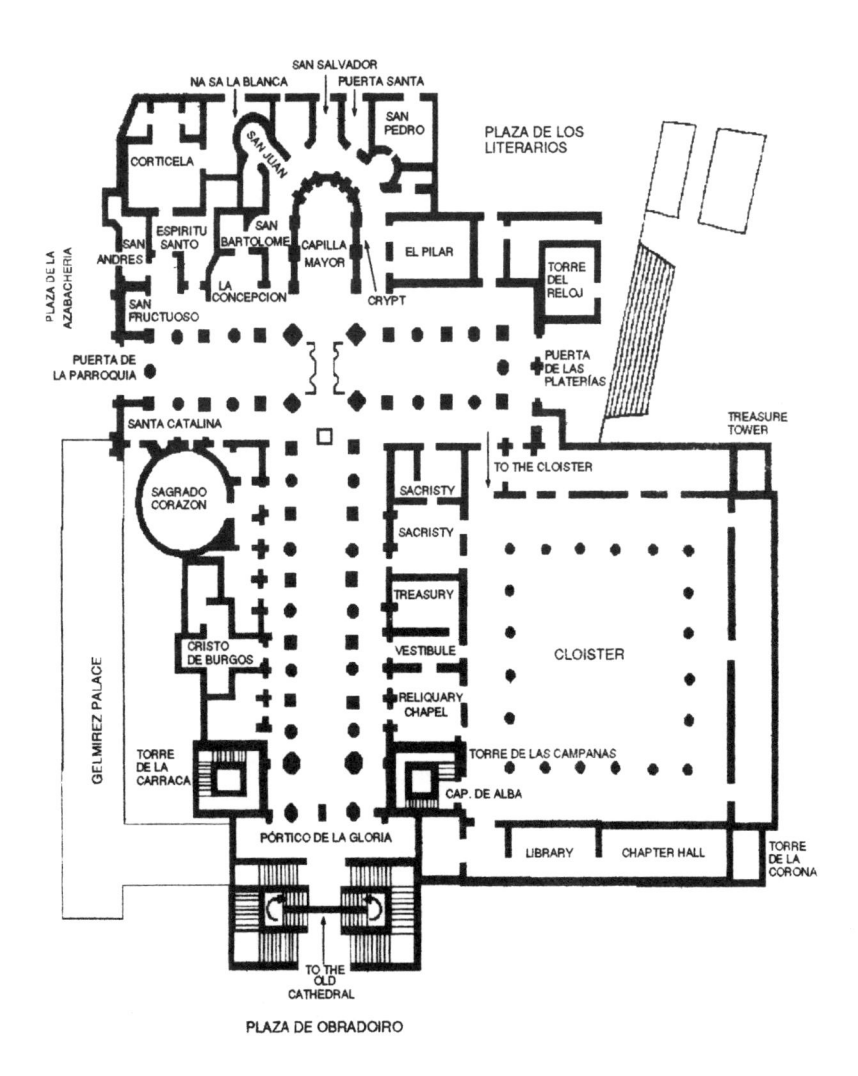

Plan of the modern Cathedral

height of a man[101]. No one can measure its external length and height. The church has nine aisles in its lower part and six in its upper part [the galleries], a large head [the apsidal chapel] containing the altar of the Saviour, a crown [the ambulatory], a body [the nave], two limbs [the arms of the transept] and eight smaller heads [chapels], in each of which is an altar.

Of the nine aisles six, as we have said, are small and three are large. The first of the large aisles extends from the west doorway to the four central piers which dominate the whole church, and is flanked by smaller lateral aisles. The other two large aisles are in the arms of the transept, one extending from the French Doorway to the central piers, the other from these piers to the south doorway; each is flanked by smaller lateral aisles. The three main aisles rise to the full height of the church, the lateral aisles only half-way up the piers[102]. Each of the main aisles measures in breadth eleven and a half times the height of a man: we take the height of a man as being eight palms[103].

---

101 Taking 1.70 metres as the height of a man (see note 103 below), these figures are reasonably close to the church's metric measurements of 94 metres (length), 63 metres (width across the transept) and 24 metres (height).

102 A very approximate translation of the Latin text, which has 'only to the *mediae cindriae*'. The meaning of this term, which is not found elsewhere—and which the author of the 'Pilgrim's Guide' may not have fully understood himself—is disputed. Professor K.J. Conant (*The Early Architectural History of the Cathedral of Santiago de Compostela*, Cambridge, Mass., 1926) suggests the translation 'to the middle of the piers'. Cf. note 105.

103 Eight palms, the height of a man, is about 1.70 metres. The

In the main aisle [the nave] there are twenty-nine pillars, fourteen on the right, the same number on the left and one between the two inner doorways at the west[104] end of the church and separating the two entrance passages. In the arms of the transept, between the French Doorway and the south doorway, are twenty-six pillars, twelve on the right, as many on the left and two inside the doorways, separating the entrance passages. In the crown [ambulatory] of the church there are eight columns surrounding the altar of St James.

The six small aisles in the upper part [the galleries] of the church are equal in length and in breadth to the small [lateral] aisles below them. On one side they are engaged in the walls and on the other they are borne on the pillars which rise from the main aisles, with twin columns rising above the level of the gallery[105]. The number of pillars in the upper part of the church is equal to the number in the lower part. Similarly the number of arches[106] in the upper part is equal to the number in the lower part; but in addition there are two twin columns between the pillars[107].

---

measurement given here approximates to the wall-to-wall width of the nave and lateral aisles (19.5 metres); the width of the nave alone ('main aisle') is just under 10 metres.
104 The Latin text, in error, has 'north'.
105 A paraphrase: the Latin text has 'twin columns, which stonemasons call *mediae cindriae*'—a phrase which suggests that the term was new to the author of the 'Guide'.
106 *Cingulae*: another term whose precise significance is unknown.
107 The text has 'twin columns, which are called *columnae cindriae* by stonemasons': again the exact meaning of the term is uncertain.

In this church there is no fissure, no defect. It is admirably built, large and spacious, clear, of fitting size, harmoniously proportioned in breadth, length and height; and it is of two storeys, like a royal palace. A man who goes up into the galleries, if he is sorrowful when he goes up, will be happy and comforted after contemplating its perfect beauty.

Of the windows

The number of glass windows in the basilica is sixty-three[108]. Above each of the altars round the ambulatory there are three; in the upper parts of the basilica round the altar of St James there are five windows, by which the altar is well lighted; and in the galleries there are forty-three windows.

Of the doorways

The church has three principal doorways and seven smaller ones. One of the principal doorways is at the west end; the others are on the north and south sides. Each of them has two entrances, and each entrance has double doors. The first of the seven smaller doorways is called St Mary's Doorway[109]; the second is the Doorway

---

108 i.e. a total of 15 in the five chapels round the ambulatory plus 5 plus 43.
109 Puerta de Santa María, between the chapels of St Nicholas (now represented only by an apse-like recess in the approach to the Corticela chapel) and the Holy Cross. It gave access to the church of Santa María de la Corticela.

of the Sacred Way[110]; the third is the Doorway of St Pelagius[111]; the fourth is the Chapter Doorway[112]; the fifth is the Stoneyard Doorway[113]; the sixth is also called the Stoneyard Doorway[114]; and the seventh is the School Doorway[115], which also gives access to the archbishop's palace.

Of the fountain of St James

When we from France desire to enter the Apostle's basilica we go in on the north side. Outside the doorway, close to the road, is the hospice of the poor pilgrims of St James, and here too, beyond the road, is a forecourt or paradise, to which nine steps lead down[116].

---

110 Between the chapels of St Faith (now dedicated to St Bartholomew) and St Nicholas; rediscovered and reopened in 1934. Not the present Puerta Santa.
111 Puerta de San Pelayo, between the chapels of the Saviour and St Peter; so called because it was used by the monks of San Pelayo de Antealtares. Now the Puerta Santa.
112 Puerta de la Canónica, in the south transept between the chapels of St Martin and John the Baptist. The site of this doorway is now occupied by the Capilla del Pilar.
113 Puerta de la Pedrera, in the south transept; probably so called because the stonemasons had their workshop in the cloister. It is now the doorway into the cloister.
114 In the wall of the south aisle. Only the arch of the doorway can now be distinguished.
115 Puerta de la Escuela, in the wall of the north aisle; probably so called because there was a school in the archbishop's palace. Here too only the arch of the doorway can be seen.
116 The Latin term is *paradisus*, which gave the French word *parvis*, the forecourt of a church. The level and the layout of the square were altered in the 18th century.

At the foot of the steps is a marvellous fountain[117] which has not its like anywhere in the world. It stands on a base with three steps, which supports a very beautiful circular stone basin, hollowed out in the form of a cup or a dish, so large that, as I believe, fifteen men could easily bathe in it. In the centre is a bronze column, broader at the base and of well proportioned height, which stands on a seven-sided stone base. On top of the column are four lions, from whose jaws flow four streams of water for the use of pilgrims and the people of the town. The water coming from the lions' mouths falls into the basin below, and from there it flows away through an opening in the basin and disappears underground. Thus it cannot be seen where the water comes from or where it goes. The water is sweet, nourishing, pure, clear, of excellent quality, warm in winter and cool in summer. Round the column runs the following inscription, written in two lines under the lions' paws:

I, Bernard, treasurer of St James, brought this water here and erected this monument, for the salvation of my soul and the souls of my parents, on 11th April 1122.

Of the city's paradise

Beyond the fountain, as we have said, is the forecourt or paradise, which is paved with stone. Here are sold the shells which are the badges of St James, and

---

117 The fountain was demolished in the 15th century. The basin, which hardly seems large enough to accommodate fifteen bathers, is now in the cathedral cloister.

also wineskins, shoes, deerskin scrips, purses, thongs, belts, all kinds of medicinal herbs and other drugs, and much else besides. Also there are on the French Road money-changers, innkeepers and divers merchants. The paradise is a stone's throw long and wide.

Of the north doorway

On the far side of this paradise is the north doorway[118] of the basilica of St James, known as the French Doorway, which has two entrances, both decorated with beautiful sculpture. On the outside of each entrance are six columns, some of marble and others of stone: three on the right and three on the left, that is six on one entrance and six on the other, making a total of twelve. On the outside wall above the column between the two entrances is the seated figure of the Lord in Majesty, giving a blessing with His right hand and holding a book in His left. Round the throne, seeming to support it, are the four Evangelists. To the right is a representation of Paradise, with another figure of the Lord reproaching Adam and Eve for their sin. To the left the Lord is depicted driving them out of Paradise. All round are figures of saints, animals, men, angels, women, flowers and other creatures, whose nature and quality we cannot describe because of their great number. In the tympanum above the left-hand entrance is a representation of the Annunciation of the blessed Virgin Mary, with the angel Gabriel speaking to

---

118 Replaced in the 18th century by the present Puerta de la Azabachería. Some of the sculpture is now on the Puerta de las Platerías: see note 119.

her. Also above the entrance on the left, to the side, are the months of the year and many other fine works of sculpture. On the outside wall are two large and fierce-looking lions, one on the left and one on the right, their eyes fixed on the doors as if guarding the entrance. On the jambs of the doorways are four figures of apostles, each holding a book in his left hand and seeming to bless those entering the basilica with his right. The left-hand door has Peter on the right and Paul on the left; the right-hand door has John on the right and James on the left. Above the apostles' heads, projecting from the jambs, are carved figures of bulls' heads[119].

Of the south doorway

The south doorway[120] of the apostolic basilica has two entrances, as we have said, and four doors. On the right-hand entrance, outside, the Betrayal of Christ is very finely carved in the first row above the doors. There our Lord is tied to the column by the Jews; there He is scourged; there Pilate sits on his throne as if judging Him. Above this, in another row, the blessed Mary, Mother of the Lord, is represented in Bethlehem

---

[119] The following pieces of sculpture from the original doorway have been identified on the Puerta de las Platerías: Christ in majesty; the expulsion from Paradise (above the left-hand doorway); perhaps the Annunciation (two barely recognisable figures on the left-hand arch); the month of November (Sagittarius, the Archer); and some other fragments. The reproving of Adam and Eve, part of the representation of February and perhaps some other small fragments are in the cathedral museum.

[120] The Puerta de las Platerías.

with her Son, together with the three kings who have come to visit the Infant and His Mother, offering their threefold gift, and the star and the angel warning them not to go back to Herod[121]. On the jambs of this entrance, as if guarding the doors, are two apostles, one on the right and one on the left; and on the jambs of the left-hand entrance there are likewise two apostles[122]. In the first row above this entrance is carved the Temptation of the Lord[123]. In front of the Lord are horrid angels, like monsters, setting Him on the pinnacle of the Temple; others offer Him stones, urging Him to turn them into bread; others show Him the kingdoms of this world, feigning that they will give them to Him if He will fall on His knees before them and worship them—which God forbid! But other pure angels, the good angels—some behind Him and some above Him—minister to Him with censers.

On the same doorway are four lions, one on the right and one on the left of each entrance. Between the two entrances, above the central pillar, are two other fierce lions, back to back[124]. The doorway is flanked by eleven columns: there are five to the right of the right-hand entrance and five to the left of the left-hand entrance, and the eleventh is between the two entrances.

Some of these columns are of marble, some of stone, finely carved with divers figures—flowers, men,

---

121 All this sculpture, some of it badly mutilated, is still in place.
122 Only one of these figures is an apostle (Andrew); the others are Moses, a bishop and a woman holding a lion. A mistake by the author of the 'Guide', perhaps influenced by the four apostles on the north doorway?
123 Still in place.   124 Still in place.

73

birds, animals. The columns are of white marble. Nor must we omit to mention the woman[125] depicted beside the Temptation of Christ, holding in her hands the stinking head of her seducer, cut off by her own husband, which, compelled by her husband, she must kiss twice every day. O what a terrible and admirable punishment for the adulterous woman, to be made known to all!

In the upper row above the four doors, towards the gallery of the basilica, is a row of figures magnificently carved of white marble[126]. The Lord stands erect, with St Peter on His left holding the keys, and the blessed James on His right between two cypresses, and St John his brother beside him, and to right and left the other apostles. Above and below, to right and left, the wall is beautifully carved with flowers and men and saints and animals and birds and fish and other figures which we cannot describe in detail. And above the entrances are four angels, each with a trumpet to announce the day of judgment[127].

Of the west doorway

The west doorway[128] with its two entrances surpasses the other doorways in beauty, size and sculptural decoration; it is larger than the others, handsomer and more finely carved. It is approached from outside by many steps, and is flanked by columns of different marbles, decorated with varied figures and

---

125 Still in place.   126 Still in place.   127 Still in place.
128 Replaced in the late 12th century by the present Pórtico de la Gloria.

devices—men, women, animals, birds, saints, angels, flowers and ornaments of all kinds. Its decoration is so rich that we cannot describe it in detail. On the highest point is the Transfiguration of our Lord as it took place on Mount Tabor, carved with magnificent skill. The Lord is seen on a white cloud, His face resplendent as the sun, His garments brilliant as snow, with the Father above Him, speaking to Him. Also seen are Moses and Elijah, who were present with Him, speaking of His death which should be accomplished in Jerusalem. There too are the blessed James, Peter and John, to whom, before all others, our Lord revealed His Transfiguration.

Of the towers of the basilica

The church will have nine towers: two above the doorway with the fountain[129], two above the south doorway, two above the west doorway, two above the spiral staircases[130] and the largest over the crossing in the centre of the basilica[131]. With these and other most beautiful works the basilica of the blessed James is resplendent in glory. It is entirely constructed of solid brown stone which is as hard as marble; the interior is decorated with varied paintings, and it is excellently covered externally with tiles and lead. Of all we have described part is completely finished; the rest remains to be done.

---

129 The north doorway.
130 Traces of these towers have been found at the angles between the nave and transepts. The staircases led down into the crypt.
131 The original lantern tower has been replaced by the present dome.

Of the altars of the basilica

The altars of the basilica[132] are arranged in the following order. First, near the French Doorway, which is to the left of the church [in the north transept], is the altar of St Nicholas[133], and next to this is the altar of the Holy Cross[134]. Then, in the crown [ambulatory], come the altar of St Faith the virgin[135]; the altar of St John, the apostle and evangelist, brother of St James[136]; the altar of the Saviour, in the largest of the chapels[137]; the altar of St Peter the apostle[138]; the altar of St Andrew[139]; the altar of St Martin the bishop; and the altar of St John the Baptist[140]. Between the altar of St James and the altar of the Saviour is the altar of St Mary Magdalene[141], in which morning masses are sung for the pilgrims. In the

---

132 The first nine of these altars correspond to the chapels ('heads') referred to on page 66—two in each arm of the transept and five round the ambulatory.
133 Dedicated to the patron of travellers and pilgrims; removed to make room for a passage giving access to the Corticela chapel.
134 Incorporated in the Capilla de la Concepción in the 16th century.
135 Since the 16th century the Capilla de San Bartolomé.
136 Now the Capilla de Santa Susana; enlarged in the 16th century, but with some remains of Romanesque work.
137 See note 99.
138 Capilla de San Pedro, now generally known as the Capilla de Nuestra Señora de la Azucena.
139 The site of this and the following chapel is now occupied by the 16th century Capilla de la Virgen del Pilar.
140 The site of this chapel is now occupied by the Puerta Real.
141 No trace remains of this altar, which lay behind the high altar.

galleries of the church are three altars[142]: the principal one is dedicated to St Michael the Archangel, the one on the right to St Benedict and the one on the left to St Paul the apostle and St Nicholas the bishop; on this side is the archbishop's chapel[143].

Of the body and the altar of St James

So far we have spoken of the characteristics of the church: we must now consider the venerable altar of the Apostle. In this venerable basilica, according to tradition, the revered body of the blessed James rests under the magnificent altar set up in his honour. It is enclosed in a marble tomb which lies within a fine vaulted sepulchre of admirable workmanship and fitting size. That the body is immutably fixed there we know from the evidence of St Theodomir, bishop of the city, who discovered it and was unable to move it from the spot. May they blush for shame, therefore, those envious people beyond the mountains who claim to have some part of it or to possess relics of it![144] For the body of the saint is here in its entirety—divinely illuminated by paradisiac carbuncles, constantly honoured by divine fragrances, radiant in the light of celestial candles and devoutly attended by watching angels.

---

142 These chapels were on the inner wall of the west front.
143 The 12th century archbishop's palace adjoined the north-west tower of the Cathedral (on the left of the west end when looking east).
144 A number of places in France and Italy, in particular Toulouse, claimed to possess relics of St James.

Over his sepulchre is a modest altar[145] which, we are told, was erected by his disciples and which, from love for the Apostle and his disciples, no one has sought to destroy; and over this is a large and beautiful altar five palms high, twelve palms long and seven palms wide. Such at any rate are the measurements I took with my own hands. The small altar lies under the larger one, enclosed on three sides—to left, right and behind—leaving the front open so that when the silver altar frontal is removed the older altar can easily be seen.

Anyone wishing, from devotion to the blessed James, to present an altar cover or cloth for the Apostle's altar should make it nine palms wide and twenty-one palms long; and anyone wishing, for love of God and the Apostle, to present a cloth to cover the front of the altar should make it seven palms wide and thirteen palms long.

Of the silver altar frontal

The altar frontal is magnificently worked in gold and silver. In the centre is depicted the throne of our Lord, surrounded by the twenty-four elders as they were seen by the blessed John, brother of St James, in his Apocalypse, that is to say twelve on the right and twelve on the left, seated in a circle and holding in their hands lutes and flasks of perfume. In the centre is our Lord, as if on a throne of majesty, holding the book of life in His left hand and giving a blessing with His right. Round the throne, and seeming to support it, are the

---

[145] Now in the museum in the convent of San Pelayo de Antealtares.

four Evangelists. To right and left are the twelve apostles, three in the front row and three above them on the right-hand side, and similarly on the left. All round are most beautiful flowers, and between the apostles are handsome columns. Along the top of this splendidly decorated frontal is the following inscription in verse:

This frontal was made by Diego II[146], bishop of St James, in the fifth year of his episcopate. It cost the treasury of St James seventy-five silver marks.

And below is this inscription:

When this work was completed Alfonso[147] was king, Raymond[148] was duke and the above-mentioned Diego bishop.

Of the canopy over the altar of the Apostle

The canopy[149] over this venerable altar is finely decorated both inside and outside with paintings, carvings and varied ornaments. It is square, borne on four columns, and harmoniously proportioned in height and breadth. Inside, on the first level, are eight figures of women, two in each corner, representing the virtues specially celebrated by Paul. Over their heads are standing figures of angels holding in their raised hands a throne in the top of the canopy. In the middle of the throne is the Lamb of God holding a cross with its foot.

---

146 Diego Gelmírez, bishop of Santiago from 1100.
147 Alfonso VI of Castile and León (1064–1109).
148 Raymond of Burgundy, Duke of Galicia.
149 Replaced in the 15th century.

Outside, on the first level, are four angels, two on the front and two to the rear, proclaiming with trumpets the resurrection of the dead on the day of judgment. On the same level are four prophets, Moses and Abraham on the left-hand side and Isaac and Jacob on the right-hand side, holding scrolls on which are written their prophecies.

Round the canopy, on the upper level, are seated figures of the twelve apostles. On the front is the blessed James, holding a book in his left hand and giving a blessing with his right, with another apostle on his right and a second on his left. Similarly there are three apostles on the right-hand and left-hand sides of the canopy and on the rear. Above this, on the roof of the canopy, are seated four angels, as if guarding the altar. At the four corners of the canopy, at the base of the roof, are the four Evangelists with their emblems.

The inside is painted, while the outside is decorated with both sculpture and painting. On top of the canopy is a small monument with three arches, carved with a representation of the divine Trinity. Under the first arch, facing west, is the Father; under the second, facing south and east, is the Son; and under the third, facing north, is the Holy Ghost. Above this again is a resplendent silver orb bearing a precious cross.

Of the three lamps

In front of the altar of St James hang three large silver lamps in honour of Christ and the Apostle. The one in the middle is of great size and is beautifully carved in the form of a large mortar. It has seven receptacles containing seven lamps, symbolising the seven gifts of the Holy Ghost. Only oil of balsam or myrtle or benzoin or olive is put in these lamps. The one in the middle is larger than the others, and on the outside of the others are carved two figures of apostles. May the soul of Alfonso, king of Aragón[150], who is said to have presented this lamp to St James, rest in eternal peace!

Of the dignity of the church of St James and its canons

On the altar of the blessed James no one celebrates mass unless he be a bishop, archbishop, pope or a cardinal of the church[151]; for in this basilica there are usually seven cardinals who celebrate the divine office on this altar. Their constitutions and privileges have been recognised by many pontiffs and confirmed in particular by Pope Callistus. This dignity which the basilica of the blessed James is fortunate in possessing may not, in love for the Apostle, be taken away from it by any man.

---

150 Alfonso VII of Castile and León (Alfonso I of Aragón), d. 1134.
151 A purely honorific title borne by seven members of the chapter of the cathedral of Santiago: a privilege originally granted by Pope Paschal II (1099–1118).

Of the builders of the church and the beginning and completion of the work

The master builders who began the construction of the basilica of the blessed James were Bernard the Old, a marvellous master, and Robert[152], aided by some fifty other builders working diligently under the direction of Wicart, Segeredo, head of the chapter, and Abbot Gundesindo, in the reign of Alfonso king of Spain and Diego I[153], a valiant knight and a generous man.

The church was begun in the year 1078. From the year in which it was begun until the death of Alfonso, the valiant and illustrious king of Aragon, there were 59 years; until the murder of Henry [I], king of England, 62 years; and until the death of Louis le Gros, king of France, 63 years[154]. From the laying of the first stone in its foundations to the laying of the last stone was 44 years. Since the time it was begun until the present day this church has been celebrated for the miracles performed by the blessed James: here health is given to the sick, the blind recover their sight, the tongues of the dumb are loosed, hearing is granted to the deaf, the lame are made able to walk, the possessed are

---

152 The names might suggest a French origin. Bernard the Old may be the treasurer of St James mentioned on page 70, or possibly his father.

153 Bishop Diego Peláez (1070–88).

154 Alfonso (VII of León and Castile, I of Aragón) died in 1134, Henry I of England in 1135, Louis VI of France in 1137. This sentence, which gives different dates for the start of work on the cathedral, is a later addition to the manuscript by another hand.

delivered, the prayers of the faithful are heard, their desires are accomplished, the fetters of sin are cast off, the sky opens to those who knock, consolation is given to the afflicted, and hosts of people from all parts of the world make their way here to bring the Lord their gifts and their praise.

Of the dignity of the church of St James

It must not be forgotten that Pope Callistus, of blessed memory, transferred to the basilica and city of St James the archiepiscopal dignity which had previously belonged to the see of Mérida, the metropolis in the land of the Saracens. He did this from love of the Apostle and in his honour, and for that purpose consecrated and confirmed Diego[155], a man of noble birth, as first archbishop of the apostolic see of Compostella. This same Diego had previously been bishop of St James.

---

[155] Diego Gelmírez, bishop of Santiago from 1100, became archbishop when the see was granted metropolitan status by Pope Callistus II in 1120.

Chapter X

Of the Number of the Canons of St James

According to tradition there are seventy-two canons attached to this church, the same number as the seventy-two disciples of Christ. They follow the Rule of the blessed doctor Isidore[156] of Spain. Each week they share the offerings made to the altar of St James. The first canon receives the offerings made in the first week; the second, those made in the second week; the third, those made in the third; and so on until the last. Every Sunday tradition calls for the offerings to be divided into three parts. The first part goes to the hebdomadary[157]; the other two parts are then divided into three; and one part is generally given to the canons for their meal, another to the church for its works and a third to the archbishop. The offerings for the week from Palm Sunday to Easter, however, go as a matter of right to the poor pilgrims of St James lodged in the hospice[158]. But in addition, if the just divine law were observed, a tenth of the offerings ought to go to the poor who come to the hospice; for all poor pilgrims should, for the love of God and the Apostle, receive full

---

156 See notes 64 and 82.
157 The 'duty canon' for the week.
158 Presumably the hospice founded in 1104 outside the north gate of the Cathedral (page 69).

hospitality in the hospice on the night following their arrival. The sick should be charitably cared for in the hospice until their death or complete restoration to health, as is the practice at Saint-Léonard[159], where all the poor who come there receive their subsistence.

In addition custom requires that offerings received at the altar from early morning to tierce on Sundays should be given to the lepers of the town.

And if any prelate of this church should commit any fraud in this matter or change the destinations of the offerings, as we have described them, he would have to answer to God for this sin.

---

[159] See pages 37-38.

Chapter XI
Of the Reception to be given to Pilgrims of St James

Pilgrims, whether poor or rich, returning from St James or going there must be received with charity and compassion; for whosoever receives them and gives them hospitality has for his guest not only St James but our Lord Himself. As the Lord says in His gospel, *'He that receiveth you receiveth me'*[160]. Many are those who have incurred the wrath of God because they would not take in the pilgrims of St James and the needy.

A weaver in Nantua, a town between Geneva and Lyons, refused bread to a pilgrim of St James who asked for it; and at once he saw his cloth fall to the ground, rent asunder. At Villeneuve a poor pilgrim of St James asked for alms, for the love of God and the blessed James, from a woman who was keeping bread under hot ashes. She told him that she had no bread: whereupon the pilgrim said, 'May the bread that you have turn into stone!' The pilgrim had left the house and gone some distance on his way when the wicked woman went to take her bread out of the ashes and found a round stone in the place where the bread had

---

160 Matthew 10,40.

been. Struck with remorse, she set out to look for the pilgrim, but could not find him.

At Poitiers two valiant French pilgrims, returning from St James in great need, asked for hospitality, for the love of God and St James, in the street running from the house of Jean Gautier to the church of Saint-Porchaire, but found none. Finally, at the last house in the street, by the church, they were taken in by a poor man; and that night, by the operation of divine vengeance, a fierce fire broke out and quickly destroyed the whole street, beginning with the house where they had first asked for hospitality and going right up to the house where they were taken in. Some thousand houses were destroyed, but the one where the servants of God were taken in was, by His grace, spared.

Thus we learn that the pilgrims of St James, whether rich or poor, should be given hospitality and a considerate reception.

Here ends the fourth book of the Apostle St James.

Glory be to him who has written it and to him who reads it.

This book was first accepted, after careful examination, by the Church of Rome.

It has been written in many places—at Rome, in Jerusalem, in France, Italy, Germany and Friesland, but principally at Cluny.

APPENDIX

Modern Guides for the Pilgrim

Eusebio Goicoechea Arrondo, *Rutas Jacobeas*. Estella, Los Amigos del Camino de Santiago, 1971.

René Brynaert, *En vacances sur le chemin de Compostelle*. Paris, Editions Duculot, 1981. (A guide mainly for motorists).

G. Bernès, G. Véron and L. Laborde Balen, *The Pilgrim Route to Compostela*. London, Robertson McCarta, 1990. (A guide for walkers).

Elías Valiña Sampedro, *The Camino de Santiago: Pilgrim's Guide*. Translated from the Spanish by Laurie Dennett. Vigo, Editorial Galaxia, 1992.

* * * * *

Booklets published by the Confraternity of St James:

Pilgrim Guide to Spain (updated annually).
    1992 Edition £2.75.
Pilgrim Guides to the Roads to Santiago de Compostela:
    1 Paris to the Pyrenees, 1992. £2.50.
    2 Arles to Puente la Reina, 1989. £2.50.
    3 Le Puy to the Pyrenees, 1991. £1.50.

Some accounts by modern travellers:

Walter Starkie, *The Road to Santiago*. London, John Murray, 1957.

Edwin Mullins, *The Pilgrimage to Santiago*. London, Secker and Warburg, 1974.

T.A.Layton, *The Way of Saint James*. London, Allen and Unwin, 1976. (With an abridged translation of the 'Pilgrim's Guide').

P. Barret and J.-N. Gurgand, *Priez pour nous à Compostelle*. Paris, Hachette, 1978; Livre de Poche, 1978. (Based largely on earlier accounts of the 14th to 18th centuries).

Rob Neillands, *The Road to Compostela*. Ashbourne, Moorland Publishing Co., 1985. (Cycling).

Laurie Dennett, *A Hug for the Apostle*. Macmillan of Toronto, 1987. (Walking).

Robin Hanbury-Tenison, *Spanish Pilgrimage: A Canter to St James*. Hutchinson, London, 1990; paperback edition, Arrow Books, 1991. (Riding).

INDEX

Abdias 51
Aegidius (Gilles, Giles), St
. . . . 29-34,35
Agde 35
Agen 36
Aimery (Aymericus) . . 11,59
Aix-en-Provence 37
Alava 24,25
Alfonso I of Aragon 11,81,82
Alfonso VI of Castile and
León 79
Alfonso VII of Castile and
León 11,81,82
Aliscamps cemetery, Arles 28
Andrew, St 50
Andrew, builder 11
Angély: . . see St-Jean d'Angély
Anjou. 38
Aragon 21
Aragón, R. 13
Arastain, king of Brittany 55
Arfaxat, magus 50
Arga, R. 13,17
Arles 27,28
Arnauld de la Guigne 20
Arnold, builder 11
Astorga 8,14
Astorito 7

Atapuerca 7
Athens 46
Augustine, St 36
Auxerre 52
Avitus, builder 11
Azabachería, Puerta de la,
Santiago Cathedral 71
Babylon 49,50
Bacchus 62
Badilo 37
Barbadelo 8
Barcelona 25
Basque language 23
Basques 19,22-25
Bayonne 19,25
Belin 55-56
Belorado 7
Benedict, St 37
Bernard the Old 82
Bernard the Treasurer 70,82
Bernesga, R. 14
Bethany 48
Biscay 24,25
Blaye 55
Bohemond 40
Borce 5,7
Bordeaux 3,17,55

Brittany 55
Brittany, Sea of 21
Burbia, R. 14
Burgos 5,7,26
Burguete 7
Burgundians. 36

Cacabelos 8,14
Caesarius (Césaire), St . . 27
Callistus II, Pope . . . .
. . . . 1,5,11,13,59,81,83
Camino, Puerta del, Santiago
. . . . 59
Campos. 26
Canfranc 7
Caprasius (Caprais), St . . 36
Carrión de los Condes . . 7,14
Carrión, R. 14
Cartagena 28
Castañeda 8
Castile 21,26
Castilians 25
Castrojeriz 7
Cathedral, Santiago de
  Compostela 62,63-86
Cea, R. 14,56
Cebrero, Monte 5,8,26
Chamalières 34
Charlemagne . . . .
. . . . 21,22,30,35,55,56
Cize 3
Cize, Pass of 3,7,13,17,19,21

Clement I, Pope 45,52
Cluny. 88
Compostella: see Santiago de
  Compostela
Conques 3,36-37
Constantinople 45
Corbigny 38-39
Cornwall 25
Coutances 34
Cross of Charles 21
Cúa, R. 14
Cuevas 14

Denmark 55
Diego, bishop: see Gelmírez,
  Peláez
Dionysius (Denis), St . . . . . .
. . . . 45-46,52
Dominic (Domingo de la
  Calzada), St 56

Ebro, R. 14
Ega, R. 13
English 25
Esla, R. 14
Estella 5,7,13,14
Ethiopia. 25
Eustella 53
Eutropius (Eutrope), St 45-54
Evurtius (Euverte), St 42,43

Facundus, St. 56
Faith (Foy), St 36-37
Fajera, Puerta, Santiago . . 59
Falgueriis, Porta de, Santiago
. . . . 59
Ferreiros 8
Florence, St 35
Foncebadón 5,8,26
Fortus, builder. 11
France 21,35,45,51,88
Francígena, Porta, Santiago
Cathedral. 59,63
French Doorway, Santiago
Cathedral 71
French Road, Santiago 62,71
Friesland 55,88
Frómista 5,7
Fronto (Front), St. 41
Fulgentius (Fulgence), St 42

Galicia. 14,21,26
Galicians 26
Galilee 47
Galilee, Sea of 47
Garin of Lorraine. 55
Garonne, R. 17
Gascons. 18
Gascony 17,18
Gellone 35
Gelmírez, Diego. . . . 11,79,83
Genesius (Genès), St 28
Geneva 87

George, priest 41
Germans 36
Germany 88
Getae. 23
Gilles (Giles, Aegidius), St
. . . . 29-34,35
Gondebaud, king of
Friesland 55
Great St Bernard 9
Greece. 30,45,52
Guiva, Queen 47
Gundesindo, Abbot. 82

Henry I of England 82
Hérault, R. 35
Herod, King 47
Herrerías. 8
Hilary (Hilaire), St 44
Honoratus (Honorat), St. . 28
Hornillos del Camino 7
Hungarians 34

Ibañeta 21
Irago, Monte 5,8,26
Isidore, St 42,57,85
Italy 88
Itero, Puente de. 7,14

Jaca 5,7
Jerusalem . . 9,37,48,49,50,88
John the Baptist, St. . . . 44-45
Julius Caesar 25

Landes 17,18,55
Larrasoaña 7
Lavacolla 15
Lavamentula 15
Lazarus 48,49
Leboreiro 8
Leizar-Athéka 3,22
Leo the heretic 44
León 5,8,14,26,57
Leonard of Limousin, St. . . .
. . . . 34,38-41
Léotard, St 38
Lepoeder, Collado. 3
Lérins 28
Limousin 38
Linares de Rey 8
Logroño 7,14
Loire, R. 43
Lorca 13
Los Arcos 7,14
Louis VI of France 11,82
Lyons 87

Macerellis, Porta de,
  Santiago 62
Mámoa, Puerta de, Santiago
  59
Mansilla de las Mulas . . 8,14
Marseilles 37
Marsile 22
Martin, St 35,43,55
Mary Magdalene, St . . 37-38

Matthew, St 26
Maximinus (Maximin), St 37
Mazarelos, Puerta de,
  Santiago 62
Mérida 83
Miño, R. 8,11,15
Modestus (Modeste), St . . 35
Moissac 3
Molinaseca 8
Monreal 5,7
Monte del Gozo 15,59
Mont-Joux 9
Montpellier 3
Mount of Joy 15

Nadabar 25
Naddaver 25
Nájera 5,7,25,56
Nantua 87
Navarre 14,23
Navarrese 13,22,23,24,25
Nicanor 48
Nîmes 31,35
Nive, R. 3
Noblat see St-Leonard de Noblat
Normans 34
Nubians 25
Numiani 25

Oca, Forest of 7,26
Oca, Mt 25
Odrón, R. 14

Ogier, king of Denmark .. 55
Oliver 22,55
Orange 35
Orbigo................ 8
Orléans 42
Ostabat 3,19

Padrón 59,62
Palas de Rey 5,8
Pamplona 5,7,13,25
Paradise, Santiago Cathedral
.... 69-71
Paris 45,52
Paschal II, Pope 81
Paul, St 27
Peláez, Diego 82
Peña, Puerta de la, Santiago
.... 59
Penne, Porta, Santiago .. 59
Périgueux 3,41
Persia 47,50
Peter, St 41,51,52
Peter, builder 11
Philip, St 50
Philip I of France 35
Phrygia 44
Pisuerga, R. 14
Platerías, Puerta de las,
  Santiago Cathedral ......
.... 71,72-74
Poitevins 17
Poitiers............ 44,87

Poitou 17,45
Ponferrada........... 8,14
Porma, R. 14
Pórtico de la Gloria, Santiago
  Cathedral 74
Presa, R. 14
Primitivus, St 56
Provence 30
Puente la Reina .. 3,5,7,13,17
Puerta Santa, Santiago
  Cathedral 69
Puertomarín 8,11,15
Puy, Le 36
Pyrenees 3

Rabanal del Camino .. 5,8,11
Raymond of Burgundy .. 79
Raymond de Soule 20
Redecilla 7,56
Rhône, R. 28,30,31
Robert, builder......... 82
Roger, builder 11
Roland........... 22,30,55
Roland, Hospice of 7,22
Romanus (Romain), St .. 55
Rome 30,51,52,88
Roncesvalles........ 7,22,55
Runa, R............... 13

Sahagún.......... 5,7,14,56
St-Eutrope, church, Saintes
.... 54

95

St-Euverte, church, Orléons
 43
St-Front, cathedral,
 Périgueux 41
St-Gilles-du-Gard 3,27,29-34
St-Guilhem-le-Désert 35
St Hilaire-le-Grand, church,
 Poitiers 44
St James: ...... see Santiago
St-Jean d'Angély 44
St-Jean de Sorde 18
St-Jean-Pied-de-Port .. 3,19
St-Léonard de Noblat ......
 3,37,38-41,86
St-Michel, Vicomte de 20
St-Michel-Pied-de-Port 5,7,19
St-Porchaire, church, Poitiers
 87
St-Romain, church, Blaye 55
St-Samson, church,Orléans
 43
St-Seine 34
St-Seurin, church, Bordeaux
 36,55
St-Thibéry, abbey 35
Ste-Croix,church,Orléons 42
Saintes 3,45,51-54
Saintonge 17
Sala de la Reina (Sala
 Regina) 8
Salt River 13

San Benito del Campo,
 church, Santiago 63
Sancto Peregrino, Porta de,
 Santiago 59
San Félix (Fiz) de Solovio,
 church, Santiago 62
San Isidoro, church, León 57
San Martín, Puerta, Santiago
 59
San Martín Pinario, church,
 Santiago 62
San Miguel 8
San Miguel dos Agros,
 church, Santiago 62
San Pedro d'Afora, church,
 Santiago 62
San Pelayo de Antealtares,
 church, Santiago 63
Santa Cristina, hospice .. 7,9
Santa María de Corticela,
 chapel, Santiago Cathedral
 63
Santa Susana, church,
 Santiago 62
Santiago de Boente 8
Santiago de Compostela
 5,8,15,20,59-86
Santo Domingo de la
 Calzada 7
Sar, R. 15,59
Saracens 22,23,83
Saracens, Castle of the 8

Saragossa 25
Sarela, R. 15,59
Sarria 8
Saturninus (Sernin), St . . 36
Scots 22,25
Segeredo 82
Severinus (Seurin), St 55
Seville 42,57
Sil, R. 14
Simón, St 50
Simon the Leper 37
Somport pass . . 3,5,7,9,13,17
Stephen, builder 11
Subfratribus, Porta de,
   Santiago 59
Susannis, Porta de, Santiago
   59

Tardajos 7
Thaddaeus,St 50
Theodomir, Bp. 77
Tiberius (Thibéry), St 35
Tiermas 7
Torio, R. 14
Torres del Río 14
Toulouse 3,17,35,36,77
Tours 3,17,42,43
Triacastela 5,8
Trinidad, church, Santiago 62
Trinidad, Puerta, Santiago 59
Trinquetaille. 28

Trophimus (Trophime), St
   27,28

Urraca, Queen 11

Valcarce 5,8,15
Valcarlos 3,22
Valley of Charles (Valcarlos)
   22
Vézelay 37-38
Viana 14
Villafranca del Bierzo 5,8,14
Villafranca Montes de Oca 7
Villanova 8
Villarente, Puente de 14
Villarroya 7
Villa Us 8
Villeneuve 87
Viscarret 5,7
Vivien d'Aigremont 20

Warradac 48
Western Sea 21
Wicart 82
William of Aquitaine 35

Xerses, Emir 47

Zaroen, magus 50
Zosimus, Pope 27

97